ELECTION MELTDOWN

DIRTY TRICKS, DISTRUST, AND THE THREAT TO AMERICAN DEMOCRACY

☑ ☑ ☑

RICHARD L. HASEN

Yale

UNIVERSITY PRESS

New Haven and London

Yale University Press books may be purchased in quantity for educational,
business, or promotional use. For information, please e-mail sales.press@
yale.edu (U.S. office) or sales@yaleup.co.uk (U.K. office).

Set in Gotham and Adobe Garamond type by IDS Infotech Ltd.,
Chandigarh, India.
Printed in the United States of America.

Library of Congress Control Number: 2019945878
ISBN 978-0-300-24819-7 (hardcover : alk. paper)

A catalogue record for this book is available from the British Library.

This paper meets the requirements of ANSI/NISO Z39.48-1992
(Permanence of Paper).

10 9 8 7 6 5 4 3 2 1

For Deborah, Shana, and Jared,
still waiting for a voting system befitting our great democracy
but seeing things getting worse rather than better

Contents

Acknowledgments

As always, I benefited greatly from the expertise and wisdom of generous readers. I thank the following people who read all or parts of the manuscript: Bob Bauer, Doug Chapin, Erwin Chemerinsky, David Ettinger, Ned Foley, Howard Gillman, Jared Hasen-Klein, Dale Ho, Steve Kay, Ron Klain, Brendan Nyhan, Norm Ornstein, Kyhm Penfil, Rick Pildes, Nick Stephanopoulos, Adam Winkler, my University of California, Irvine, colleagues who participated in a faculty workshop, and the anonymous readers for Yale University Press. Thanks also to Joan Biskupic, Jackie Calmes, Jill Grinberg, Justin Levitt, and Hunter Walker for useful comments and suggestions. Although the book is much improved thanks to early readers, I take full responsibility for remaining errors.

Thanks to Bill Frucht of Yale University Press, who encouraged me to pursue this project and improved it greatly with his suggestions, to Karen Olson at the press for help with all manner of logistical issues, to Robin DuBlanc and Margaret Otzel for excellent production assistance, and to my agent Melissa Flashman, whose smarts and initiative helped bring this book to life.

Julia Jones provided excellent research assistance, with additional cite-checking help from Hannah Bartlett, Tim Duong, Jack Feinfield, and Sabrina Van Der Linden-Gonzales. Stacy Tran provided professional and terrific administrative assistance, and Ellen Augustiniak, Dianna Sahhar, and Christina Tsou provided first-rate library support.

Most of all, I thank my wife, Lori Klein, for her excellent comments on the manuscript as well as her unwavering support, sage advice, love, and patience. Her support makes everything possible. This book is dedicated to our most successful joint endeavors.

Some of the material in this book appeared in altered form in some earlier writing of mine. I gratefully acknowledge permission to reprint parts of these works:

Donald Trump Was Just Handed a Chance to Supercharge Voter Suppression in 2020, Slate, Jan. 8, 2019, https://slate.com/news-and-politics/2019/01/donald-trump-voter-suppression-plan-2020.html

Race or Party?; How Courts Should Think about Republican Efforts to Make It Harder to Vote in North Carolina and Elsewhere, 127 Harvard Law Review Forum 58 (2014), https://harvardlawreview.org/2014/01/race-or-party-how-courts-should-think-about-republican-efforts-to-make-it-harder-to-vote-in-north-carolina-and-elsewhere/

Race or Party, Race as Party, or Party All the Time: Three Uneasy Approaches to Conjoined Polarization in Redistricting and Voting Cases, 59 William and Mary Law Review 1837 (2018)

The 2016 U.S. Voting Wars: From Bad to Worse, 26 William & Mary Bill of Rights Journal 629 (2018)

Vote Suppressors Unleashed, Slate, Nov. 27, 2017, https://slate.com/news-and-politics/2017/11/donald-trump-will-supercharge-voter-suppression-if-the-rnc-consent-decree-falls.html

The Voting Wars: From Florida 2000 to the Next Election Meltdown (Yale University Press 2012)

Why Democrats Should Not Call the Georgia Governor's Race "Stolen," Slate, Nov. 18, 2018, https://slate.com/news-and-politics/2018/11/georgia-stacey-abrams-brian-kemp-election-not-stolen.html.

Thanks to David Smiley for permission to republish his photograph of the Broward County, Florida, 2018 ballot; to the Associated Press for permission to publish an altered version of Damian Dovarganes, AP Images, *California Hispanics*, http://www.apimages.com/metadata/Index/California-Hispanics/41af1e6fdfec4e45adcc2efdcb e6e571/36/0 (August 15, 2012); and to Jeff Giesea, who posted portions of the leaked Project Birmingham "After-Action Report."

Occasionally I altered capitalization and eliminated internal quotation marks for clarity. Check the original source before quoting secondary sources here. I saved endnote references for the end of a paragraph. Paragraphs containing quotations without citation refer to material cited in the earlier notes.

Election Meltdown

The New Voting Wars

"Mr. President, why haven't you condemned . . . the North Carolina election fraud? This is a big story. The Republican candidate is calling for a new election. Why have you not condemned that, given you've condemned other kinds of voter fraud?"[1]

Hallie Jackson, chief White House correspondent for *NBC News*, queried President Donald J. Trump during a February 2019 opportunity for press questions in the Oval Office before a trade meeting between U.S. and Chinese government officials. Just a day earlier, Mark Harris, a Republican congressional candidate who was 905 votes ahead of Democrat Dan McCready in the uncalled 2018 race for North Carolina's Ninth Congressional District, surprisingly agreed to McCready's call for a new election. He did so after a North Carolina election board heard overwhelming evidence that one of Harris's consultants, Leslie McCrae Dowless Jr., had engaged in illegal campaign activities such as forging absentee ballots. For Harris, who had spent many weeks demanding that the board declare him the winner and claiming that "the Democrats and liberal media have spared no expense disparaging my good name," it was a change of heart.[2]

At the election board hearing, Harris's son John, an assistant U.S. attorney, had testified about emails he had sent his father. Before his father hired Dowless, John warned that the consultant appeared to have engaged in illegal ballot activities during previous elections.

Harris's legal team had not turned those emails over to the board, but John did. Four times, Harris said under oath that he did not recall if he told anyone whether he expected those emails to be made public. After a hasty recess called by his attorney, Harris changed his tune: he said he had discussed those emails with another son a few days before the hearing. Then, citing health reasons, Harris joined McCready's call for a new election and left the board hearing just before he was to be cross-examined under oath by Democratic attorney Marc Elias. Elias said he thought Harris's team stopped the testimony "to spare Harris of potentially giving further answers that would expose him to legal jeopardy." The board unanimously called a new election.[3]

The reporter's question to Trump was prompted by the president's relentless and unproven past claims of massive voter fraud committed by Democrats. Without evidence, he had charged that millions of noncitizens voted in the 2016 elections. He had claimed that voter impersonation fraud, where one person goes to a polling place and votes in another's name, was a major problem, despite all evidence to the contrary. He had accused Brenda Snipes, a Democratic election official in Broward County, Florida, of trying to steal the 2018 U.S. Senate election from Republican Rick Scott, who was challenging incumbent Democratic senator Bill Nelson. But Trump had been silent about the North Carolina race, the first credible case in decades of criminal conduct potentially affecting the outcome of a federal election.[4]

Trump's meandering answer to Jackson was full of unsupported claims:

PRESIDENT TRUMP: Well, I condemn any election fraud. And when I look at what's happened in California with the votes, when I look at what happened—as you know, there was just a case where they found a million fraudulent votes. When I look at what's happened in Texas—

Q: There haven't been those cases. This is an actual case, sir.

PRESIDENT TRUMP: Excuse me. Excuse me. When I look at what's happened in Texas. When I look at that catastrophe that took place in Florida where the Republican candidates kept getting less and less and less and less. And fortunately, Rick Scott and Ron [DeSantis] ended up winning their election, but it was disgraceful what happened there.

So I look at a lot of different places all over the country. I condemn any voter fraud of any kind, whether it's Democrat or Republican—or when you look at some of the things that happened in California, in particular. When you look at what's happened in Texas with all of those votes that they recently found were not exactly properly done, I condemn all of it. And that includes North Carolina, if anything—you know, I guess they're going to be doing a final report. But I'd like to see the final report. But any form of election fraud, I condemn.[5]

Trump's reluctance to comment on the North Carolina chicanery until there was a "final report" to show "if anything" untoward had happened contrasted with his rush to judgment in cases involving what he perceived as Democratic malfeasance. Trump's reference to Florida was about Brenda Snipes's incompetence in running the 2018 elections, which I consider in chapter 2. It is enough to say here that Florida law enforcement officials found absolutely no evidence of criminal activity in Broward County's conduct of those elections.

The reference to the "million fraudulent votes" in California appeared to be based upon a viral Facebook post falsely claiming that 1.7 million unregistered people had voted in the state. Some people attributed the post to the conservative group Judicial Watch, but the group denied having anything to do with it. "Not ours," a Judicial Watch spokesperson told *PolitiFact.* "Just some random person misinterpreting."[6]

The "random person" was apparently "misinterpreting" questionable data from a Judicial Watch lawsuit claiming millions of ineligible people were registered on California's voter rolls. The lawsuit aimed to force Los Angeles County and the state to remove up to 1.5 million inactive voters from rolls. The people targeted included those who had died or moved but were not taken off the rolls. Judicial Watch claimed those inactive voters presented a risk of fraud, but it did not show that anyone had voted in the ineligible voters' names. The suit was settled with no admission of wrongdoing and an agreement by election officials to contact those on the inactive list to determine their status.[7]

Trump's allusion to "what's happened in Texas with all of those votes that they recently found were not exactly properly done" appears to refer to a sloppy attempted purge of supposed noncitizens from the Texas voter rolls in 2019. Texas's attorney general, Ken Paxton, indicted years ago on securities fraud charges but not yet tried, had sent a "VOTER FRAUD ALERT" in a January 2019 tweet, claiming there were ninety-five thousand noncitizens on Texas's voter rolls, including fifty-eight thousand who had supposedly voted in Texas elections.[8]

Though Paxton's post was retweeted nearly thirty-five thousand times and "liked" nearly eighty-three thousand times, Texas officials were quick to walk back the figures. A list of supposed nonvoters that Texas provided to counties, which administered voter registration lists, contained thousands of errors, including many Texans who were naturalized citizens and eligible to vote. Nearly 1 million Texas residents had become naturalized citizens between 2007 and 2016, and so a list

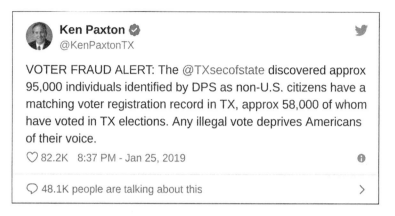

Ken Paxton ✔
@KenPaxtonTX

VOTER FRAUD ALERT: The @TXsecofstate discovered approx 95,000 individuals identified by DPS as non-U.S. citizens have a matching voter registration record in TX, approx 58,000 of whom have voted in TX elections. Any illegal vote deprives Americans of their voice.

♡ 82.2K   8:37 PM - Jan 25, 2019   ⓘ

♡ 48.1K people are talking about this   ›

Texas attorney general Ken Paxton tweet, January 25, 2019

of people who were once noncitizens could not accurately identify current noncitizens.

The state offered no evidence to support its wild claim of fifty-eight thousand noncitizens voting, much less that there was significant noncitizen voter registration. As the *Washington Post*'s Philip Bump noted, such claims usually fell apart on closer inspection: "A similar effort in Florida targeted 180,000 people—and ultimately removed 85 from voter rolls. Eighty-five people, not 85,000." The Texas case led to numerous lawsuits arguing that the purge effort was meant to suppress the votes of the state's Latino population, and scuttled the legislative confirmation of Texas's interim secretary of state, David Whitley, who ended up taking a job in the Texas governor's office. Texas abandoned the effort to use the list as the basis for a voter purge and agreed to pay $450,000 in plaintiffs' attorneys' fees.[9]

In granting a preliminary injunction to stop Texas counties from using the faulty lists to purge voters, U.S. district court judge Fred Biery wrote: "The evidence has shown in a hearing before this Court that there is no widespread voter fraud. The challenge is how to ferret the infinitesimal needles out of the haystack of 15 million Texas voters. . . . The Court further finds and concludes the Secretary of State, though perhaps unintentionally, created this mess. As Robert Fulghum taught in *All I Really Need to Know I Learned in Kindergarten*, 'always put things back where we found them and clean[] up our own messes.' "[10]

President Trump's barely coherent statement about North Carolina and election fraud in the course of answering a few press questions in front of a foreign dignitary, and his brushing aside of a reporter's appeal to reality—"There haven't been those cases. This is an actual case, sir"—illustrate all four of the principal dangers facing American elections and democracy in 2020 and beyond: voter suppression, pockets of electoral incompetence, dirty tricks in elections, and a rising incendiary rhetoric about "stolen" or "rigged" elections. Each of these phenomena tends to undermine voters' trust in the fairness and accuracy of American elections.

First, we have seen an escalation in the use of *voter suppression* by Republican legislatures and election officials as a tool to reduce turnout of likely Democratic voters. While at first these post-2000 efforts were somewhat haphazard and of uncertain significance, events such as the Supreme Court's 2013 decision in *Shelby County v. Holder,* which killed off a key provision of the Voting Rights Act, have accelerated the pace of suppressive laws. Actions like Texas's move to cull the voter rolls based on unsubstantiated claims of voter fraud fit into this pattern.[11]

As the courts have become less protective of voting rights, we can expect more suppressive laws even as arguments that such laws are needed to combat phantom voter fraud have collapsed under the weight of the evidence. And these attempts at suppression motivate Democrats to express skepticism about the fairness of elections. Chapter 1 tells much of the story through a look at Trump's failed "voter fraud" commission headed by notorious vote suppressor Kris Kobach, and a related trial in Kansas regarding the state's illegal law requiring documentary proof of citizenship for voting, which left Kobach with egg on his face.

Second, pockets of *incompetence in election administration* have enabled both Democrats and Republicans to raise cries of rigged or stolen elections that appear increasingly credible to hardcore partisans. Even though most election administrators are doing an admirable and professional job, often under serious resource constraints, in close elections it is the weakest link among those who run elections that matters most. The problem happens with some frequency in large American cities, which are often controlled by Democrats.

In Florida, Broward County's elected Democratic election administrator, Brenda Snipes, had a history of poor performance before the 2018 Senate race appeared to come down to Broward. In earlier elections, she had improperly destroyed ballots, left measures off the ballot, delayed reporting voting results, and mixed up provisional ballots with regular ones. Scott had to sue to get Snipes to reveal how many ballots remained to be counted in the Senate race.

Snipes was not the only inept administrator. Georgia's Republican secretary of state, Brian Kemp, did a terrible job maintaining the security of the state's voter registration database. He then added malfeasance to his misfeasance by attempting a cover-up, falsely accusing both the U.S. Department of Homeland Security and the Georgia Democratic Party of "hacking" into the election system. He put the latter unsupported charge on the front page of his official Georgia Secretary of State website that Georgia voters used to access voting information in the days before the 2018 election, in which he was running to be the state's governor. Kemp's actions threatened the integrity of the vote in Georgia.

Third, old-fashioned and newfangled *dirty tricks* undermine both the integrity of the vote and its appearance. These days, concerns about foreign and domestic interference hang over the American voting system. We know some of what Russian government agents did to probe state voter registration databases and manipulate public opinion via social media in 2016. But the Russians were simply trendsetters, and we got a taste of the future when we saw Democratic operatives try to sway the 2017 U.S. Senate special election in Alabama toward Democrat Doug Jones and away from Republican Roy Moore using social media tools that emulated those used by Russia in 2016. Such attempts will no doubt grow more sophisticated as technology improves, but anyone can post false information today on Twitter or Facebook, usually with no repercussions. That Trump was apparently taken in by a fake Facebook post about fraudulent votes in California, or at least used it to deflect attention from actual election crimes in North Carolina benefiting a Republican candidate, is as unsurprising as it is demoralizing.

There is every reason to believe that both foreign and domestic actors will try to use dirty tricks in the run-up to the 2020 elections, particularly since Donald Trump's presence stirs strong emotions and distrust on both sides. Such tricks may attempt to alter outcomes directly or to inflame passions and undermine confidence in the fairness of the election. At the worst, they could include manipulation of the American power grid or other critical infrastructure to directly interfere with the casting or counting of votes.

But not all dirty tricks require high-tech methods or use of social media. McCrae Dowless allegedly bought, stole, and altered absentee ballots on behalf of Mark Harris in North Carolina's Ninth Congressional District race by paying cash, which a former employee said some of his desperate workers then used to buy drugs. Especially in local races and places without a watchful independent media presence, low-tech dirty tricks remain a real concern.[12]

Fourth is the concern about *incendiary rhetoric*. Donald Trump and others in the Republican Party have ratcheted up the rhetoric about Democrats stealing elections, raising the prospect that if Trump loses a close contest in 2020, he could refuse to concede. We saw a test run of this strategy in 2018, when Trump alleged that Broward's Brenda Snipes was trying to cheat to give the lead in Florida's Senate race back to Nelson. It wasn't just Trump and it wasn't just Florida. Florida senator Marco Rubio suggested Democrats were trying to steal the election by waiting for a full counting of the votes, even though the counting followed the procedures set by state law. Speaker of the House Paul Ryan suggested there was something "bizarre" in the fact that Republicans were ahead in many U.S. House races in California on Election Night, before Democrats pulled ahead when millions of legitimate absentee and other ballots were counted in the weeks after the election.[13]

Especially worrisome on the Republican side is that 2020 will be the first election since the 1980s in which the Republican National Committee will be freed from a court order that had limited "ballot security" measures, which were aimed at minority voters and alleged to be racially discriminatory. The decree was put in place when, among other things, Republican officials sent off-duty police officers to the polling places in New Jersey in the 1980s. The officers wore armbands that read "National Ballot Security Task Force," and some carried two-way radios and firearms. In 2020, Trump may try to have the Republican Party "protect" the polls by intimidating minority voters.[14]

Democrats have ratcheted up the rhetoric too, calling the Georgia election "stolen" because of Republican suppression efforts. While many of Georgia's actions were questionable and unjustified, there was no good evidence that they determined the outcome, and such language wrongly put the focus on whether suppression affects election outcomes rather than on whether the state may put stumbling blocks in front of voters for no good reason.

And as much as Democrats worry that Trump won't concede a close election if he can raise unsubstantiated claims of voter fraud, what will Democrats do if they are on the losing side of a close election that they can credibly claim was marked by efforts of voter suppression? Few things are more important to democratic legitimacy than the losers' acceptance of the results of elections, yet this new rhetoric shows that the country's faith in elections, which we have long taken for granted, may be fraying.

The synergy of these four factors—voter suppression, pockets of incompetence, foreign and domestic dirty tricks, and incendiary rhetoric—undermines public trust in the fairness and accuracy of American elections and creates high risks for the 2020 elections and beyond. The concluding chapter of the book suggests immediate, medium-term, and long-term changes to minimize the chances of an election meltdown threatening the stability of American democracy. The issue is especially challenging when one of greatest risks to the integrity of the process comes from the sitting president of the United States.

Immediate steps to take at the moment of a disputed election include a public convening of bipartisan elders to vouch for the fairness of the electoral process and the legitimacy of the winner; resort to the courts, including the U.S. Supreme Court, to resolve election disputes over the rightful winner; and mass public protests to force the losing party to concede and move on. The bad news is that none of these steps is likely to be successful in a protracted conflict over election results.

This makes pursuit of medium- and long-term solutions all the more urgent. The medium-term solutions are tied to the four threats to public trust in elections identified in the book. As to voter suppression, I call for continued lawsuits and public protests against states' efforts to make it harder to register or vote for no good reason, and a complete rejection by the media, election professionals, elected officials, and public intellectuals of claims that voter fraud is a major problem in U.S. elections. As to election administrator incompetence, greater federal guidance on good election practices and a concerted effort to root out poor election administrators must be a priority, especially in large cities where the task of conducting elections is complex and the large number of ballots means that extra time is needed to process votes.

As to dirty tricks, a reinvigorated U.S. Election Assistance Commission, working with the Department of Homeland Security and state and local governments, must take steps to prevent the hacking of election databases and machinery as well as critical infrastructure affecting the conduct of elections, such as the power grid. The government must require greater disclosure of who is spending money to influence elections via social media, and it must strengthen laws barring foreign interference in elections. The public must pressure social media companies to do better at combating the spread of misinformation. And prosecutors need to take steps to stop rare but dangerous election crimes, as in Bladen County, North Carolina. As for overheated rhetoric, the more that is done to strengthen the election system in the other three areas, the more likely it is that the public will reject irresponsible claims of "stolen" or "rigged" elections.

Finally, in the longer term, we need to improve both the structure of our election process and our civics education, so that future American elections are less vulnerable to mistrust, manipulation, and malfeasance. First, the United States should join other advanced democracies in moving toward nationalized, nonpartisan election administration, as well as implement automatic voter registration for all eligible voters with a national identity card to be used for voting. Such a system must not place any significant burdens on voters, and it must give voters a way to prove identity if the card is not available. Second, we must renew civics education for adults and children, fostering discussions across platforms and venues about the importance of the rule of law, democratic legitimacy, and the peaceful transition of power, including discussions of the danger of speaking about "stolen" elections without any proof or even basis in reality.

The point of this book is not to ask whether American democracy can survive Donald Trump. Trump is more a symptom of the American electoral system's malfunction than a cause. The problems will exist even after he leaves the political scene. Nor is this book a broader attack on issues of the equality of voting power, such as the use of the Electoral College for choosing the president or the presence of partisan or racial gerrymandering.

The point instead is to ask about the resiliency of an electoral system that most people have long taken for granted. Trump certainly has been a norm-breaker, and his actions have opened a national conversation about whether it is norms rather than law that hold American democracy together.

The central norm at stake in this book is the peaceful transition to power after hard-fought but fair elections. Nothing before Trump guaranteed such transitions, and nothing in the Trump or post-Trump era guarantees it either. Democracy takes work, and it begins through recognition of the stresses on the American system of producing clear and fair winners and losers.

Very close elections always put the electoral system under stress. But the country has repeatedly survived that stress, most recently in the disputed 2000 election culminating in the Supreme Court's decision in *Bush v. Gore* and the immediate decision by Democrat Al Gore to concede defeat to Republican George W. Bush. Many Democrats viewed the process as unfair to Gore, and many Republicans viewed it as unfair to Bush.[15]

Bush v. Gore happened before the rise of social media and Trumpism. Since then, stress on the system has increased dramatically. We have to act now to take steps so that the next time there is a razor-thin election—and there will be one, sooner or later—our civil society is strong enough to withstand foreign and domestic efforts to tear us apart.

1

The Icicle

"Just hypothetically, Dr. Richman, if you came across the name Carlos Murguia, would you code that as foreign or non-foreign?"

It was March 2018, and Dale Ho, who directs the American Civil Liberties Union's voting rights project, had just asked one in a series of extraordinary questions in his cross-examination of expert witnesses for the state of Kansas in arguably the most important voting rights trial so far in the twenty-first century. In the case, *Fish v. Kobach*, a federal district court in Kansas was considering whether the threat of noncitizen voting in Kansas elections justified a state law that required people registering to vote to provide documentary proof of citizenship, such as a birth or naturalization certificate. In most other states, signing a statement affirming citizenship under penalty of perjury is proof enough. The ACLU was concerned that the Kansas law would not prevent a significant amount of noncitizen voting but would disenfranchise many eligible Kansans who could not produce the necessary papers. Before the court suspended the law, roughly thirty thousand people had their registrations rejected or put on hold because of the new requirement.[1]

Kris Kobach led Kansas's defense team. Kobach, then serving as Kansas's secretary of state, is one of the country's leading public figures contending that voter fraud is a major problem in the United States. He was one of a small group of public figures I previously dubbed the "fraudulent fraud squad," who built up the myth of rampant voter fraud that Republican legislatures have used to justify severe rules making it harder to register and vote. President Trump has parroted this myth repeatedly at MAGA rallies and elsewhere. Among prominent election officials and scholars, Kobach is the only one who backed Trump's evidence-free assertion that potentially millions of fraudulent votes were cast in the 2016 presidential election.[2]

At trial, Kobach took the unusual step of personally heading the legal team defending Kansas's law rather than allowing the state's attorney general's office to do so. A former law professor at the University of Missouri–Kansas City, Kobach examined and cross-examined witnesses, eventually not only losing the case but facing sanctions for misleading the court, for disobeying an earlier court order to make sure that eligible voters could register while the case was pending, and for "flaunting [flouting] disclosure and discovery rules that are designed to prevent prejudice and surprise at trial." A magistrate judge fined Kobach $1,000 for misleading the court, and the state of Kansas had to pay the ACLU's attorney's fees spent trying to get Kobach to comply with the earlier court order. After the trial, the judge required Kobach to take continuing legal education courses on the rules of evidence or civil procedure. He eventually had his staff use a state-issued credit card to pay the $1,000 fine and the $359 cost of his online continuing education course on civil trial fundamentals.[3]

The significance of the trial was not lost on those who follow the voting wars, the fights exploding in the last few decades between those who state that voter fraud is a major problem and those who consider voter suppression the real concern. Fraudulent fraud squad members such as the Heritage Foundation's Hans von Spakovsky, who served as one of Kobach's expert witnesses, had been arguing for years about the supposed scourge of voter fraud, and in the *Fish* case their claims were finally put to the test in a court of law bound by neutral rules of evidence. Presiding over the case was Julie A. Robinson, the chief judge of the Federal District Court for the District of Kansas, a fourth-generation Kansan and the first African American on that court when appointed in 2001 by President George W. Bush.[4]

The case ended up in Judge Robinson's courtroom after a series of motions and appeals had already resolved many of the complex legal issues it presented. Kansas had passed its law requiring documentary proof of citizenship as a prerequisite to voter registration in 2013, and the ACLU and others contended the law violated both the Constitution and parts of the National Voter Registration Act that Congress passed in 1993. One provision of the NVRA, also known as the "motor voter" law, required that states offer voters the ability to register to vote for federal elections when applying for a driver's license. The law mandated that state DMVs require drivers to provide no more than the minimal information necessary to ensure voting eligibility, and the form had to include a portion in which a voter attested to citizenship under penalty of perjury.[5]

Kobach and Kansas argued that the attestation requirement was not enough to prevent noncitizens from voting, and that despite the federal motor voter law, the part of the Constitution granting each state the power to set the qualifications for voters gave Kansas the right to require registrants to show documentary proof of citizenship. The argument fit well with Kobach's political position as a hardliner on illegal immigration: not only were people illegally coming to the country, they were voting (and no doubt voting overwhelmingly for Democrats). Challengers to the Kansas law argued that the motor voter law preempted it and that it violated the Constitution's Equal Protection Clause by discriminating against voters lacking easy access to documents proving citizenship.

Eventually, the U.S. Court of Appeals for the Tenth Circuit held that Kansas could require documentary proof of citizenship for people registering at the Kansas DMV only if it could prove that despite the attestation requirement, "a substantial number of noncitizens [had] successfully registered," and that requiring documentary proof was the least intrusive way to verify voter citizenship eligibility. When the case got back to the trial court, the two main questions the court had to resolve were whether a substantial number of noncitizens had registered in Kansas under the old law, and whether the new law was so burdensome on some voters as to be unconstitutional.[6]

Studies had found very little evidence of noncitizen voting, and the number of prosecutions and convictions for noncitizen voting was small. In the extensive News21 database of election crime prosecutions and convictions across the United States from 2000 to 2012, noncitizen voting accusations made up only 2.8 percent of cases, just fifty-six out of more than two thousand. Those fifty-six cases resulted in two convictions and seventeen plea deals. Kobach had successfully lobbied the Kansas legislature to give him the power to prosecute voter fraud, a power unique among state chief election officers. He nonetheless prosecuted only nine cases of voter fraud through 2017, and he earned only one conviction for noncitizen voting, from a legal (not illegal) immigrant. At least seven of his cases involved prosecutions of Republicans over the age of sixty, some of whom voted both in Kansas and in another state where they owned a second home or other property.[7]

Despite the lack of prosecutions even as Kobach scoured the state looking for noncitizen voter fraud, Professor Jesse Richman of Old Dominion University published a report claiming that up to thirty-two thousand noncitizens in Kansas were registered to vote under the old system. Kobach then chose Richman as an expert witness for the state, no doubt because his was the only peer-reviewed study suggesting such an astonishing rate of noncitizen voting—somewhere between thirty-eight thousand and 2.8 million voters nationally. Richman's article, coauthored with Gulshan A. Chattha and David C. Earnest and published in *Electoral Studies* in 2014, described the rate of noncitizen voting as so high that it might have been responsible for Barack Obama's winning the presidential election in 2008, as well as for passage of the Affordable Care Act, thanks to the election of Al Franken over Norm Coleman in the 2008 U.S. Senate race in Minnesota, which briefly gave Democrats a filibuster-proof majority in the Senate.[8]

At trial, using a methodology similar to what he had used in his study, Richman concluded that up to thirty-two thousand noncitizens in Kansas had registered to vote. He based his figures on self-reported voting and citizenship status in a nationwide public opinion survey called the Cooperative Congressional Election Study. Between 2006 and 2012, fourteen self-reported noncitizens in Kansas answered the CCES survey, and four of them reported voting. Richman applied the 4/14 rate reported in the sample to the 114,000 adult noncitizens in Kansas to reach the 32,000 noncitizen voters figure.[9]

One wonders how Richman's paper got published. His methodology was deeply flawed because of the very small sample size, his failure to verify the citizenship status of the fourteen self-reported noncitizens in the CCES samples for Kansas, the fact that some citizens mistakenly report their citizenship status on surveys, and the tendency of people to overreport their voting. Harvard government professor Stephen Ansolabehere, a founder of CCES and one of the nation's leading political scientists, testified that Richman misused the CCES data and that the correct interpretation showed a noncitizen voting rate approaching zero. Ansolabehere had published a peer-reviewed response to Richman explaining his errors. Richman's *Electoral Studies* analysis was so flawed that two hundred political scientists signed an open letter criticizing it.[10]

At trial, Richman offered three other ways to estimate the amount of noncitizen voting. One method found a rate of zero, which Richman unsurprisingly discounted. The other approaches had serious methodological flaws. One of his studies sampled a population of Kansas residents who had their voter registrations put on hold because they lacked documentary proof of citizenship. From this "suspense" list, he and his assistants tried to identify "foreign sounding" names to determine whether the list was excluding large numbers of noncitizens from registering. He admitted that this methodology required making "subjective" judgments.[11]

The ACLU's Dale Ho asked Richman why he had coded some Kansas residents on the suspense list with the last name "Lopez" as foreign and others not, but he did not get a good answer. Then Ho continued with a devastating line of questioning:

Q. Just hypothetically, Dr. Richman, if you came across the name Carlos Murguia, would you code that as foreign or non-foreign?
A. I'm sorry, could you, please, spell the name.
Q. Sure. Carlos, C-a-r-l-o-s, Murguia, M-u-r-g-u-i-a.
A. Probably.
Q. Probably what?
A. Probably would code it as foreign.
Q. Okay. Are you aware that Carlos Murguia is a United States District Court Judge who sits in this courthouse?
A. I am not.[12]

This was social science at its worst. Unfortunately for Kobach and his team, Richman was their strongest expert witness. Hans von

Spakovsky fared even worse on the stand against Ho. Although von Spakovsky identified himself as an expert on election administration and on questions of voter fraud, he had a law degree but possessed no social science graduate degree, admitted that he had written no peer-reviewed studies on election administration, and said he had "no idea" whether the methods he used for studying voter fraud comported with accepted social science standards. Despite claiming to be an expert, he could not identify anyone else in the country whom he considered an expert on noncitizen voting. He said he was not aware of any voter registration rules anywhere in the United States that were burdensome to voters.[13]

Von Spakovsky had a serious credibility problem. I learned about it years ago while writing my 2012 book, *The Voting Wars*. I had been searching for proof of a single case since the 1980s, anywhere in the United States, in which someone tried to steal an election through impersonation fraud—the only kind of fraud strict voter ID laws are designed to prevent. It is an exceedingly dumb way to steal an election, because one would have to hire people to go to the polls claiming to be someone else, hope that the people being impersonated had not yet voted, hope that the people being paid to commit felonies would actually cast a secret ballot the way the payer wants, and repeat this process undetected on a large enough scale to sway an election. It is no surprise that the News21 database covering a dozen years contained only ten possible *individual* cases of such fraud, and none involving a conspiracy to steal an election. Election law professor Justin Levitt found thirty-one possible impersonators casting votes out of over a billion votes cast in the United States between 2000 and 2014, and he has since come up with two recent cases of possible attempted coordinated voter fraud via impersonation.[14]

I had no luck finding any such case while researching my 2012 book, but von Spakovsky claimed there was proof of impersonation

fraud in an unpublished grand jury report of an investigation of the
Board of Elections in Brooklyn in the 1980s. He would not share
the report with me, so I could not confirm or refute his findings. He
later explained his refusal by saying to the *New Yorker*'s Jane Mayer,
"What am I—his research assistant?" Once I finally got hold of the
report, I saw that it did not offer any proof of impersonation fraud,
only of election crimes committed by election officials and party
bosses, not by voters.[15]

Von Spakovsky was no more credible as a witness in the Kansas
case. Attempting to prove a rise in voter fraud, his pretrial expert report partly relied on a 2012 news story from an NBC television affili-
ate in Florida about 100 people who were excused from jury duty
because they were not citizens, yet who were on the voting rolls. But
he admitted on cross-examination that he had not told the court
about a follow-up investigation, which showed that at least 35 of the
people on NBC's list in fact had documentary proof of citizenship.
(While it does not appear that NBC followed up with the others, in
2012 the Florida secretary of state released a list of 180,000 potential
noncitizens to be considered for purging. After investigation, just
85 people were removed from voting rolls as noncitizens. At the time,
Florida had about 12 million registered voters.)[16]

Then there was the case of the Somali American voters von Spakovsky erroneously accused of voter fraud. Ho asked:

Q. Mr. von Spakovsky, in 2011 you wrote an op-ed asserting that
a 2010 election in Missouri that ended in a one-vote margin of
victory included 50 votes cast illegally by the citizens of Somalia.
Correct?

A. Correct. But it turned out apparently that was incorrect, which is
why I did not include it in my expert report.

Q. Okay. Not talking about your expert report. I just want to talk about that op-ed for a second. You wrote that op-ed claiming that 50 non-citizens from Somalia voted in an election in Missouri, despite the fact that a month earlier there had been an election challenge—there had been an election contest in that case and a state court in Missouri issued an opinion, *Royster versus Rizzo*, finding that no fraud had taken place in that election. Correct?

A. I don't know when that opinion was issued. I wasn't aware of that when I wrote the piece, which was based on other reports.

Q. You're aware of that now, right, Mr. von Spakovsky?

A. I'm aware of that now.

Q. You never published a written retraction of your assertion about Somali[] voters illegally participating in that election, right, Mr. von Spakovsky?

A. I don't believe so, but I don't recall when I discovered that.[17]

The truth was even worse than Ho's cross-examination revealed. Von Spakovsky's 2011 op-ed, syndicated in newspapers across the U.S., stated, "A 2010 election in Kansas that ended in a one-vote margin of victory included 50 votes cast illegally by citizens of Somalia." The day it appeared, I pointed out on my Election Law Blog that the disputed election took place in Missouri, not Kansas, and that a Missouri court specifically rejected the losing candidate's claim that Somali citizens had illegally voted in the election. The next day, the op-ed appeared in more newspapers, now saying the incident happened in Missouri, not Kansas, but repeating the lie about illegal votes. Von Spakovsky had corrected the name of the state in his op-ed by, at the latest, the day after he wrote it. But no retraction for his more substantive error has run at the time I write these words.[18]

Before the trial, both von Spakovsky and Kobach had described the noncitizen voting so far discovered in Kansas and elsewhere as merely the "tip of the iceberg." Ho suggested that the two had coordinated their messaging, but whether or not they did, *Fish v. Kobach* was their chance to reveal the iceberg for all to see. If tens of thousands, maybe millions, of noncitizens were voting in the United States, and Kobach had been empowered to prosecute it in Kansas, there should be some evidence of this massive fraud. But he had nothing to show.[19]

In an opinion issued a few months after the trial, Chief Judge Robinson found that Kansas's documentary proof of citizenship law imposed a serious burden on the state's voters. She credited the testimony of plaintiffs' expert Michael McDonald that the burden fell most heavily on the young and those unaffiliated with a political party, and she noted that tens of thousands of Kansans had had their voter registration applications put on hold or rejected.[20]

She further concluded that the burden on these would-be voters was unjustified. There was likely a minuscule amount of noncitizen voting in Kansas, but the few reports of potential noncitizen voting were more likely the result of administrative error or misunderstanding of the law than attempted felonies. "Evidence that the voter rolls include ineligible citizens is weak. At most, 39 [non]citizens have found their way onto the Kansas voter rolls in the last 19 years. And, as [plaintiffs' expert] Dr. [Eitan] Hersh explained, given the almost 2 million individuals on the Kansas voter rolls, some administrative anomalies are expected. In the case of Kansas, this includes 100 individuals in [the state database] with birth dates in the 1800s, and 400 individuals with birth dates after their date of registration."[21]

"There is no iceberg," the judge concluded, "only an icicle, largely created by confusion and administrative error."[22]

Kobach's previous foray into the voter fraud fever swamp during the Trump era was the "Presidential Advisory Commission on Election Integrity." President Trump established this commission to back up his unsupported claims of massive voter fraud, which he advanced as the reason Hillary Clinton won the popular vote in the 2016 presidential election. Trump named Vice President Mike Pence the nominal chair of the commission, but Kobach, the vice chair, was the driving force behind its operation. Kobach ran the commission meetings and seemed to dictate its agenda. Trump had established the commission in May 2017, but the following January, before the start of the *Fish v. Kobach* trial, he dissolved it with none of its work completed. It never issued a report.[23]

Trump's commission to deal with phantom voter fraud looked like nothing that had come before it. After the 2000 election debacle that culminated in the Supreme Court case of *Bush v. Gore*, former presidents Jimmy Carter and Gerald Ford headed a blue-ribbon bipartisan commission looking for ways to improve the elections process. After more problems at the polls in 2004, Carter and former Republican secretary of state James Baker headed another commission. After long lines and still more problems in 2012, President Obama established a commission headed by his campaign lawyer, Bob Bauer, and Mitt Romney's campaign lawyer, Ben Ginsberg. Each of these commissions was led by a prominent Democrat and a prominent Republican, with bipartisan representation and a professional staff. They received expert advice from the top social scientists in the United States studying elections.[24]

The Bauer-Ginsberg commission, aided by its research director, Stanford law professor Nate Persily, issued a set of bipartisan proposals for shortening lines at the polls, ensuring that voter registration rolls were accurate, and making sure that eligible voters would be able to vote in an efficient way. It was no accident that Brian Britton, vice president of Global Park Operations and Initiatives at Walt Disney World Company and an expert in queue management at Disney's theme parks, sat on the commission.[25]

It was clear from the beginning that Trump's commission was different. We will return to candidate Trump's race-tinged and fact-free comments about voter fraud in chapter 4. But as soon as Trump took office, his administration removed from government servers, without explanation, the website and research of the Bauer-Ginsberg commission. In May 2017, he announced his new commission to look into voter fraud. Gone was bipartisan balance: the Republican Pence was appointed chair and the Republican Kobach was vice chair.[26]

The names of the commissioners were rolled out over weeks rather than announced all at once, as had been done with the other commissions. Eventually, four of the most notorious proponents of the myth of rampant voter fraud—Kobach, von Spakovsky, J. Christian Adams, a former Department of Justice lawyer, and former Ohio secretary of state Kenneth Blackwell—all joined. The Lawyers' Committee for Civil Rights under Law dubbed them "President Trump's Four Horsemen of Voter Suppression."[27]

Adams, a frequent *Fox News* guest who warned of the dangers of voter intimidation by repeatedly citing the actions of a couple of "New Black Panthers" at a single Philadelphia polling place in 2008, now headed the Public Interest Legal Foundation. Among its other activities, PILF issued a report warning of an "alien invasion," complete with an illustration of "a 1950s-style flying saucer approaching bucolic Virginia," and giving the names of purported noncitizens on the Virginia voting rolls. Some of those falsely named "noncitizens" sued Adams for defamation, and Adams apologized to settle the suit. Blackwell was perhaps best known for his decision in 2004, which he later reversed under pressure, to have Ohio election officials reject some voter registration forms because the applications were not printed on heavy enough paper.[28]

I myself received a shout-out from Adams in documents released in litigation after the commission closed. In an email exchange with von Spakovsky and some PILF employees at the time of the commission's founding, Adams commented on my earlier criticism of their work perpetuating the voter fraud myth: "Rick Hasen is a raw enemy activist. . . . He is the central organizing location of our foes. He is going to get very ugly toward me and Hans when/if we are nominated by the President to the Voter Fraud Commission." Logan Churchwell, the spokesperson for PILF, urged Adams to "push" my "buttons" so I would become "unhinged." "Sick of him being the elder statesman in the eyes of the MSM [mainstream media]."[29]

When fully constituted, the commission had seven Republicans and five Democrats. Three of the five Democrats were unknown nationally in the election administration field. The other two were Bill Gardner, the secretary of state in New Hampshire, and Matt Dunlap, Maine's secretary of state. Some Democrats who had long viewed Gardner with suspicion thought their doubts were confirmed when he agreed to serve on the commission. Dunlap claimed he joined in order to watch the process from the inside, a stance several election experts, including me, thought was naïve, but he later played a key role in the commission's downfall.[30]

We later learned from partially redacted documents, released through a Freedom of Information Act request, that the lack of partisan balance on Trump's voter fraud commission was a feature and not a bug. Before Trump named any members, von Spakovsky sent an email, which later got forwarded to Attorney General Jeff Sessions, laying out the case for excluding Democrats, academics, and "mainstream

Date: February 22, 2017 at 7:36:03 PM CST
To: "Mr. Charles J. Cooper" (b) (6)   , Ed Haden

Cc: Christian Adams (b) (6)
Subject: voter fraud commission

Chuck, Ed,

Christian got a very disturbing phone call about the voter fraud commission that Vice President Pence is heading. We are told that the members of this commission are to be named on Tuesday. We're also hearing that they are going to make this bipartisan and include Democrats. There isn't a single Democratic official that will do anything other than obstruct any investigation of voter fraud and issue constant public announcements criticizing the commission and what it is doing, making claims that it is engaged in voter suppression. That decision alone shows how little the WHouse understands about this issue.

There are only a handful of real experts on the conservative side on this issue and not a single one of them (including Christian and me) have been called other than Kris Kobach, Secretary of State of Kansas. And we are told that some consider him too "controversial " to be on the commission If they are picking mainstream Republican officials and/or academics to man this commission it will be an abject failure because there aren't any that know anything about this or who have paid any attention to this issue over the years.

Christian and I are concerned that this commission is being organized in a way that will guarantee its failure. We are astonished that no one in the WH has even bothered to consult with us or John Fund despite the fact that the three of us have written more on the voter fraud issue than anyone in the country on our side of the political aisle. I think you know from the white paper we sent you that based on our experience we have thought long and hard about what needs to be done.

(b) (6)   My cell is (b) (6)   if you need to
reach me.

Hans von Spakovsky
Manager, Election Law Reform Initiative and Senior Legal Fellow
Institute for Constitutional Government
The Heritage Foundation
214 Massachusetts Avenue, NE
Washington, DC 20002

heritage.org<http://heritage.-org>

_____

_____-__

CONFIDENTIALITY: This email and any attachments may be confidential and/or privileged and are therefore protected against copying, use, disclosure or distribution. If you are not the intended recipient, please notify us immediately by replying to the sender and double deleting this copy and the reply from your system.

Email from Hans von Spakovsky, February 22, 2017 (with redactions by the government and additional redactions of personal information by the author)

Republicans" from the commission. He and Adams were offered spots on the commission soon after.[31]

Once it got going, the commission immediately ran into problems. Kobach directed staff to request individual voter registration records from each state, including names, addresses, dates of birth, and Social Security numbers. Apparently he meant to look for registered noncitizens by comparing those data to citizenship records at the Department of Homeland Security. Many states balked.

Some Democratic officials expected the matching procedure to be flawed and suspected the commission's work would be used as a pretext for tougher federal or state voter registration rules. California secretary of state Alex Padilla released a statement reading in part: "California's participation would only serve to legitimize the false and already debunked claims of massive voter fraud made by the President, the Vice President, and Mr. Kobach. The President's Commission is a waste of taxpayer money and a distraction from the real threats to the integrity of our elections today: aging voting systems and documented Russian interference."[32]

Some Republican officials thought the federal request was an intrusion on state sovereignty. Before he even received the commission's letter, Mississippi secretary of state Delbert Hosemann said in a statement: "They can go jump in the Gulf of Mexico and Mississippi is a great state to launch from. . . . Mississippi residents should celebrate Independence Day and our state's right to protect the privacy of our citizens by conducting our own electoral processes." Colorado citizens began canceling their voter registrations after the state agreed to comply with the request because they did not want the Trump administration to have access to their data. They reasoned that they could use Colorado's same-day registration policy to reregister whenever they wanted to vote.[33]

Then there were the lawsuits. Common Cause and others sued the commission for violating the Privacy Act, which bars government collection of sensitive personal information under certain circumstances. The suits eventually led to the destruction of all collected voter data after the commission disbanded. Other suits argued that the commission's rules violated the federal Paperwork Reduction Act as well as various state laws protecting the privacy of voter information.[34]

Maine secretary of state Dunlap, one of the two prominent Democrats on the commission, sued it for violating a federal law governing transparency and fairness in the operation of presidential advisory commissions. He and other commissioners alleged that Kobach was acting in secret and without input from Democratic commissioners. Dunlap won and eventually obtained several commission documents he had not been allowed to see—which he then publicly posted. The released documents showed that even before they joined the commission, von Spakovsky and Adams were providing specific suggestions to Kobach and commission staff (but not its Democratic members) about the exact information to request from each state regarding its voter registration practices. The documents also show the commission never uncovered any evidence of significant voter fraud. The failure to find evidence supporting the need for laws to combat noncitizen voting and voter impersonation is the only plausible reason for the commission's lack of transparency.[35]

The members met only twice. After their first official opening meeting, in Washington, D.C., in July 2017, they met in September 2017 in New Hampshire, where they were hosted by Secretary of State Bill Gardner. In that meeting, Kris Kobach presented and then walked back unsupported assertions he had first floated on the *Breitbart* website, that bused-in Massachusetts residents illegally voted in the Granite State.

Another meeting was planned for late January 2018, but President Trump pulled the plug on the entire enterprise, blaming "endless legal battles at taxpayer expense" and lack of cooperation from Democrats. He did not mention Republican resistance or Mississippi secretary of state Hosemann's suggestion about local swimming spots. Kobach told *Breitbart* that the effort to find evidence of noncitizen voting would continue at the Department of Homeland Security, without Democratic interference and lawsuits: "The investigation will continue, and it will continue more efficiently and more effectively. . . . By throwing their food in the air, they just lost their seat at the table." He told NPR that he would remain as an "outside adviser" on the project. That announcement was quickly rebuffed by DHS officials, who said Kobach would play no role. As far as we know, DHS conducted no subsequent investigation of noncitizen voting.[36]

One White House adviser, or perhaps it was Vice President Pence himself, told CNN that the commission was a "s[hi]t show" that had gone "off the rails." The adviser suggested that the vice president's "team . . . should have seen that assignment as a s[hi]t sandwich and treated it like a book report. . . . Avoid trouble, cite real instances of voter fraud, address structural and technology problems, make recommendations and move on."[37]

The collapse of the Pence-Kobach fraud commission and the *Fish v. Kobach* trial were watershed moments in the modern history of voter fraud mythmaking and attempts at voter suppression. For years, people like Kobach and von Spakovsky had spun stories of voter fraud by relying upon anecdotal accounts, innuendo, falsehoods, and accusations that almost never panned out. Most of this cheap talk was not subjected to cross-examination or rigorous study. The trial and commission fiasco changed all that.

The only rational conclusions to be drawn from these two episodes are that voter fraud is extremely rare, and that spurious claims more likely serve as a pretext for passing laws aimed at making it harder for people likely to vote for Democrats to register and to vote. Kobach rejected this premise, telling NPR's Robert Siegel after the collapse of the commission that "critics were making a bizarre and frankly idiotic argument. They were claiming that by looking at the issue of voter fraud, that was going to cause state legislatures to pass laws that would, in their view, make voting more difficult."[38]

But it was Kris Kobach, meeting with Trump during the 2016 presidential transition period, who used false claims of massive voter fraud as a basis for recommending legislation amending the federal motor voter law to allow states to require documentary proof of citizenship before voting. And the commission that Trump picked Kobach to head was designed to provide cover for such legislation. A sharp-eyed AP photographer captured a picture of Kobach holding a briefing outline after his meeting with Trump that included that recommendation; the $1,000 fine Kobach later received in the *Fish* case was for misleading the court and the ACLU about the outline's content. He apparently had modeled his proposed amendment to match what the ACLU, in a 2016 legal brief, wrote that the motor voter law would have to look like if it in fact allowed Kansas to require documentary proof of citizenship before voting.[39]

Fish and the commission's work showed that noncitizen voting and voter impersonation fraud weren't icebergs, or even icicles. They were puddles that evaporated in the sunlight of public inspection and legal examination.

Alas, the intellectual collapse of the voter fraud myth has done little to slow down the pace of laws, passed almost exclusively in Republican states, that make it harder to register and vote. Instead, green lights from the Supreme Court have accelerated the pace and deepened the reach of these laws, even as lawsuits and the commission's failure undermined their premises, and even as some lower courts have rejected or softened some of the more extreme attempts. According to a Brennan Center survey, twenty-five states enacted new restrictions on voting and registration from 2010 to 2018: "14 states have more restrictive voter ID laws in place (and six states have implemented strict photo ID requirements), 12 have laws making it harder for citizens to register, seven cut back on early voting opportunities, and three made it harder to restore voting rights for people with past criminal convictions."[40]

Consider the experience of North Carolina, a state at the epicenter of the voting wars given the close division between Democrats and Republicans, and with a large, mostly African American minority population. From the late 1960s through 2013, forty of North Carolina's one hundred counties were subject to the "preclearance" part of the federal Voting Rights Act, which required jurisdictions with a history of racial discrimination in voting to get approval from the U.S. Department of Justice or a three-judge federal court in Washington, D.C., before changing their voting rules. The federal government approved voting changes only if the jurisdiction could establish that the changes would not make protected minority voters worse off.[41]

In 2013, the Supreme Court put an end to this preclearance requirement in *Shelby County v. Holder*. The Court held that this part of the Voting Rights Act exceeded Congress's power to enforce the Constitution's Fourteenth Amendment, which provides equal protection of the laws, and the Fifteenth Amendment, which bars racial discrimination in voting. Writing for the five conservative justices on the Supreme Court, Chief Justice John Roberts recognized a new right of states to "equal sovereignty," holding that Congress could not require preclearance absent proof of current continued racial discrimination in voting. The majority complained that for some decades, Congress had not updated the coverage formula dictating which states needed federal approval for voting changes. This was a fair point. But the majority erred in believing (or at least stating) that "things have changed in the South" enough that preclearance was no longer necessary. Justice Ruth Bader Ginsburg wrote a dissent for the four more liberal justices, lamenting that "throwing out preclearance when it has worked and is continuing to work to stop discriminatory changes is like throwing away your umbrella in a rainstorm because you are not getting wet."[42]

Justice Ginsburg was right that the law served as a deterrent and that bad behavior would quickly return upon its removal. Within hours of the *Shelby County* decision, Texas announced it would immediately enforce its law requiring those wanting to vote to provide one of a limited number of types of photographic identification. Student IDs were unacceptable, but concealed handgun permits were allowed. Before *Shelby*, a federal court had put Texas's law on hold under the preclearance rules because the state could not prove the law would be nondiscriminatory.[43]

A few months later, North Carolina passed probably the largest package of voting rights rollbacks in a single law since before the 1965 passage of the Voting Rights Act. A majority-Republican General Assembly (the name of North Carolina's legislative body) passed House Bill 589 over staunch Democratic objections following a Democratic presidential victory in 2008 and a closely contested 2012 presidential race. The bill included a strict voter identification provision. It cut a week off early voting, used by up to 70 percent of African American voters in 2012, and barred local election boards from keeping the polls open after 1 p.m. on the final Saturday before the election. It eliminated same-day voter registration and opened up the precincts to "challengers," who could slow down voting at polling places and dissuade voters from showing up in the first place. It eliminated preregistration of sixteen- and seventeen-year-olds in high schools. It provided that a voter who votes in the wrong precinct (perhaps because of a poll worker's error) would have her or his whole ballot thrown out—the earlier law had allowed such ballots to count for those races in which the voter was eligible to vote.[44]

With preclearance gone, the legal road to block the law—under other provisions of the Voting Rights Act or the Constitution—was arduous. As the cases were pending, North Carolina softened the voter identification provision by allowing prospective voters to swear under penalty of perjury that they faced a "reasonable impediment" to getting one of the allowable forms of ID. The district court refused to put any of the challenged provisions on hold pending a trial on the merits, a decision reversed in part by the U.S. Court of Appeals for the Fourth Circuit, and then reversed again for the 2014 elections by the Supreme Court. The district court then held two trials considering voluminous evidence and issued a mammoth ruling rejecting all of the plaintiffs' arguments, including the claim that North Carolina enacted its law with racially discriminatory purpose. The trial court viewed North Carolina as having nondiscriminatory, good government purposes in passing the law, including the prevention of voter fraud and preserving public confidence in the integrity of the election system. It further determined that North Carolina's seeking data on the impacts of parts of the law on different racial groups was not evidence of intentional racial discrimination, but instead was explainable on nondiscriminatory grounds, namely, the need to assure compliance with the Voting Rights Act and the Constitution.[45]

The Fourth Circuit reversed the trial court, holding that the court committed a clear error in rejecting the plaintiffs' argument that

North Carolina passed House Bill 589 with racially discriminatory intent. Rather than seeing the state legislature as passing the law on nondiscriminatory grounds, the appellate court viewed the evidence as suggesting only partisan grounds, and the court then equated the partisan grounds to racial grounds: "Although the new provisions target African Americans with almost surgical precision, they constitute inapt remedies for the problems assertedly justifying them and, in fact, impose cures for problems that did not exist."[46]

The Fourth Circuit concluded that "the district court erred in accepting the State's efforts to cast this suspicious narrative in an innocuous light." It took a darker view of the legislature's use of racial data. The North Carolina General Assembly, it said, had engaged in intentional racial discrimination in passing the law with a partisan aim, even if its members harbored no racial animus. "The totality of the circumstances—North Carolina's history of voting discrimination; the surge in African American voting; the legislature's knowledge that African Americans voting translated into support for one party; and the swift elimination of the tools African Americans had used to vote and imposition of a new barrier at the first opportunity to do so—cumulatively and unmistakably reveal that the General Assembly used [the law] to entrench itself. It did so by targeting voters who, based on race, were unlikely to vote for the majority party. Even if done for partisan ends, that constituted racial discrimination." The challenged parts of HB 589 could not be enforced.[47]

The North Carolina story might seem like evidence that the system worked, and that courts can see through "good government" pretexts for suppressive voter efforts and block laws deemed discriminatory. But the North Carolina experience is an anomaly, and we can expect similar laws to get approval from the Supreme Court in 2020 and beyond.

To begin with, only a procedural quirk kept the case out of the Supreme Court, which, had it taken up the case, might well have reversed the court of appeals and preserved the law. While the case worked its way through the courts, Roy Cooper, a Democrat, replaced Republican Pat McCrory as North Carolina's governor. Cooper and the state's new Democratic attorney general Josh Stein sought to withdraw North Carolina's petition for Supreme Court review of the decision striking down the law. Although the state legislature protested that it had the power to seek Court review, the Court declined to hear the case, with Chief Justice Roberts issuing a rare statement explaining that the denial was because of confusion over who in North Carolina had authority over the case and not on the merits of North Carolina's argument.[48]

There's no getting around the fact that judges appointed by Democratic or Republican presidents tend to see the issue of voter suppression differently. President George W. Bush appointed Thomas Schroeder, the trial judge who upheld House Bill 589. Democratic presidents appointed the three judges on the Fourth Circuit who reversed the trial judge. The Supreme Court, filled with conservatives appointed by Republican presidents, has been more willing to uphold laws making it harder to vote, from Indiana's strict voter identification law to Ohio's law making it easy to "purge" voters from rolls if they have not voted in a couple of elections. It is not that these judges and justices are blindly following the interest of their political parties; it is that they tend to have the same worldview as others in their party, and Democrats and Republicans tend to see the voting wars differently. With Justice Brett Kavanaugh solidifying the Court's conservative majority, and Chief Justice Roberts now the "median" justice, voting rights supporters likely won't be so lucky next time, unless Roberts tempers his views to maintain the Court's bipartisan legitimacy.[49]

Second, the fight in North Carolina over restrictive voting rules was hardly over after this case. In 2018, when North Carolina Republicans had already lost their majority in the state supreme court and were at risk of losing their supermajority in the General Assembly, Republican legislators put on the ballot a proposed amendment to enshrine voter identification requirements in the state constitution. The amendment passed with 55 percent support, and the Democratic-majority state supreme court by definition could not overturn a constitutional amendment as violating the state constitution. The 2018 elections saw North Carolina Republicans lose their supermajority on the General Assembly, but in their lame duck session they passed legislation implementing the voter ID amendment over Governor Cooper's veto. The cycle of lawsuits began anew.[50]

Third and most important, North Carolina's demography provides alternative avenues of attack on restrictive voting laws that are not available in many other states. Thanks to the state's large minority population, voting rights activists could attack voting restrictions in the state using both the Voting Rights Act and the parts of the U.S. Constitution that bar racial discrimination.

These arguments are hard to make in Kansas, for example, with its much smaller minority population and where those most burdened by the state's restrictive voting law were the young and voters unaffiliated with a political party. Nor could they be made in Indiana, which was one of the earliest states to pass a strict voter identification law. In 2008 in *Crawford v. Marion County Election Board,* the Supreme Court rejected a challenge arguing that the law unconstitutionally discriminated against the poor and others who would have the most trouble obtaining voter identification.[51]

Once again, the judges and Supreme Court justices in *Crawford* divided along ideological lines. The trial judge, Reagan-appointed

Sarah Barker, rejected a constitutional challenge to the law, faulting the ACLU for not presenting evidence of voters who wanted to vote but would have trouble getting the right identification.[52]

Appellate judges also divided by party. Reagan-appointed Seventh Circuit judge Richard A. Posner wrote an opinion for the appeals court describing the law as imposing only a slight inconvenience on voters and therefore raising no constitutional problem. But to Seventh Circuit judge Terence Evans, a Carter appointee, the key fact in the case was that Indiana had never had an instance of impersonation fraud it could point to as a basis for the law, which had passed on a party-line vote. He opened his dissent from an appeal of Judge Barker's ruling with: "Let's not beat around the bush: The Indiana voter photo ID law is a not-too-thinly-veiled attempt to discourage election-day turnout by certain folks believed to skew Democratic."[53]

Posner was wrong about the burdens the laws imposed. Under the Indiana law, if you were too poor to get the documents needed for an identification card, you could file a "provisional ballot," which election officials would put aside rather than count. If you wanted your vote actually counted, you would have to make a trip, at your own expense, to a county office (which could be thirty miles or further away) to fill out a "Declaration of Indigency." And it wouldn't be enough to do this just once—you had to do it in *every election* in which you lacked the right form of identification. If you were too poor to pay for a birth certificate, it did not seem likely that you could afford the expense of getting to the county seat to have your vote counted.[54]

By 2013, Judge Posner had recognized his error and changed his tune about his vote in the *Crawford* case. He wrote in his book *Reflections on Judging*, "I plead guilty to having written the majority opinion (affirmed by the Supreme Court) upholding Indiana's requirement that prospective voters prove their identity with a photo ID—a law now widely regarded as a means of voter suppression rather than fraud prevention."[55]

The Supreme Court upheld the law on a 6–3 vote. Despite the lack of evidence that impersonation fraud was a problem in the state or that the law tended to instill voter confidence (social science evidence showed that such laws did not), it was enough for Indiana to show the law had the potential to prevent fraud or instill voter confidence.[56]

The six-justice majority divided into two camps. Three justices, led by John Paul Stevens, joined by Chief Justice Roberts and Anthony Kennedy, held that the antifraud purpose sufficed to block a challenge to the law as a whole. But these justices left open the possibility that discrete groups of voters who faced greater burdens obtaining identification could challenge the constitutionality of the law as applied to them. Three of the most conservative justices—Antonin Scalia, joined by Samuel Alito and Clarence Thomas—said it would not matter even if there were evidence of some people disenfranchised by the law, so long as *most people* did not face a serious burden. In other words, under the Scalia camp's approach, Indiana's law could be applied even against those for whom getting the right identification imposed a serious burden.[57]

Crawford was a terrible precedent, setting an awful double standard for challenging voting restrictions under the Constitution: a state need not offer actual evidence of fraud to sustain a law restricting voting, but voting rights activists must demonstrate concrete and serious burdens to convince courts to strike the laws down.

Proving that voter ID laws suppress overall turnout remains difficult, and the effects of these laws are still difficult to measure. One of the most important recent studies, by Enrico Cantoni and Vincent Pons for the National Bureau of Economic Research, showed little effect of voter identification laws on either voter turnout or the amount of fraud. Part of the reason voter identification laws don't appear to depress turnout is that Democrats mobilize to counter the effects of these laws, diverting important resources from campaigning to making sure their eligible supporters can vote.[58]

But state voter ID laws come in lots of varieties, and often the problem is with the particular types of identification that are accepted or with the specifics of implementation. For example, consider North Dakota in the 2018 elections. The state changed its voter identification law to require that voters show proof of a residential street address. That may not sound like a burden to most voters, but it did burden one particular group: Native Americans living on Indian reservations, most of whom lacked residential street addresses and whose support had been crucial in electing Democratic U.S. senator Heidi Heitkamp. After going all the way to the Supreme Court but failing to block the requirement, tribal leaders scrambled to create new identification cards that could be used for voting, and turnout surged as Native American voters fought disenfranchisement. Thus the question is not just whether a state has a voter identification law but the particulars of how it operates and whom it burdens.[59]

Moreover, voter ID laws are just one of many types of restrictive voting laws, and they are far from the most worrisome. For example, approximately thirty thousand voters in Kansas were denied the right to register to vote because of the documentary proof of citizenship law, which prevented no detectable amount of noncitizen voting.

As the laws have gotten stricter, some courts have taken to requiring states to "soften" their laws to allow exceptions, and some states have done so voluntarily to forestall lawsuits or avoid liability. In Texas, for example, signing a "reasonable impediment" affidavit affirming identity is now a way to get around not having the right identification.[60]

This softening works a lot better in theory than in practice. Most polls are staffed by volunteers who do not understand the intricacies of such rules. And voters often are not educated about their alternatives. Many Texas voters do not know that they may file an affidavit if they can't produce the right form of identification. In Georgia in the 2018 elections, many voters whose registrations were put on hold because their registration information had a minor discrepancy from official records (such as a missing hyphen in a last name) did not know that they still could go to the polls and cast a regular ballot if the name on their registration application had a "substantial match" to their official records.[61]

In Wisconsin, whose voter ID law has recently been the subject of numerous state and federal lawsuits, or Kansas, which required documentary proof of citizenship until a lawsuit stopped the practice, groups work tirelessly with the marginalized and with those facing the greatest burdens in getting the right documentation to register and to vote. The group VoteRiders, which uses volunteers to help people facing special burdens to get IDs, released recordings of three different officials at DMV offices giving a homeless man incorrect information about how to obtain a temporary identification to vote. Bureaucratic mistakes, and perhaps even intentional acts disenfranchising voters who had been promised "free IDs," have become a disturbingly common problem, despite court orders and rules relaxing the strictest requirements.[62]

Reflecting on her loss in the 2016 presidential election, including a narrow loss in Wisconsin, Hillary Clinton told a group at a 2017 conference in California, "The best estimate is that 200,000 people in Wisconsin were either denied or chilled in their efforts to vote." Others, including Democratic U.S. senator Tammy Baldwin, made the same claim: Wisconsin's strict voter identification law cost Clinton the state in the 2016 election. The nonpartisan fact-checking organization PolitiFact rated Clinton's statement "mostly false," but that did not stop her from making a similar, if tamed, version of her claim in her 2017 memoir, *What Happened*. Clinton likely found it comforting to think that something other than her campaign was to blame for losing states like Wisconsin, which were thought to be firmly in the Democratic column.[63]

The Clinton line of attack is troubling for two reasons. First, in many cases the social science evidence simply does not support firm conclusions about how restrictive voting laws affect turnout. We know such laws make it harder for some people to register and to vote, and we know such laws disproportionately fall upon people of color, who tend to vote for Democrats. But it is very difficult to say that a restrictive voting law alone made the difference in turnout in any particular election, which could be affected by factors ranging from candidate outreach to other races on the ballot to the weather. Arguments like Clinton's leave open the counterargument that the effects of attempts at voter suppression are unproven, allowing the claim that voter suppression is an icicle no more substantial than the icicle of voter impersonation.[64]

But more important, a focus on whether suppressive voting laws are changing results puts the emphasis in the wrong place, making it seem that voter suppression matters only if it affects election outcomes. Instead, we should focus on voters' dignity, and the right of each voter to register and to cast a ballot that will be fairly and accurately counted. Some voters should not have to jump a series of hurdles that others do not. Tribal leaders in North Dakota should not have to scramble for printers to make last-minute tribal identification cards with residential street addresses complying with state law absent evidence of fraudulent voting among tribal members using fraudulent addresses. The state should have to offer a good reason, and not a myth, to support a restrictive voting law, and the courts should (though there is no reason to believe they will) flip the *Crawford* script and require states to prove that their restrictive laws serve a real interest.

Clinton is hardly the only Democrat pointing to suppressive voting laws as a reason to question the fairness and legitimacy of the election. Even if such laws do not have the intended effect, Democrats focus on the bad intentions in passing them, and it is not surprising that they are sometimes too quick to blame losses on their opponents' concerted efforts to make it harder for Democrats' supporters to vote. But the asymmetry is clear: only one party is seeking to make it harder to register and vote for those likely to vote for the other party.

The bankruptcy of the claims of rampant voter fraud did nothing to impede these claims. In early 2019, the Texas attorney general Ken Paxton issued a "voter fraud alert," declaring that up to fifty-eight thousand noncitizens voted in Texas, an announcement that coincided with the increase in Latino voter turnout in the state. Right after Paxton made the announcement, President Trump tweeted: "58,000 non-citizens voted in Texas, with 95,000 non-citizens registered to vote. These numbers are just the tip of the iceberg. All over the country, especially in California, voter fraud is rampant. Must be stopped. Strong voter ID! @foxandfriends." Trump did not issue any corrective when, as was inevitable, Texas quickly walked back its claims, which relied upon faulty data. The early evidence suggested that almost none of the fifty-eight thousand people on Paxton's list were noncitizens.[65]

Kris Kobach ran for governor of Kansas in 2018, barely winning a primary against the incumbent Republican governor, Jeff Colyer, who took office when President Trump nominated Kansas's governor Sam Brownback to an ambassadorship. After public pressure, Kobach stepped aside as secretary of state from overseeing a potential recount of his own primary race.[66]

During the general election, Kobach's opponents unsuccessfully tried to get Judge Robinson to publicly release the video of Kobach's deposition in *Fish v. Kobach,* which, according to *Kansas City Star* reporter Bryan Lowry, "shows Kobach to . . . appear uncomfortable during some portions of the deposition, rubbing his eyes and crossing his hands as the ACLU peppered him with questions." The video had been played in court, but the court allowed release of only a transcript. Even without the video, Kobach lost the governor's election to Democrat Laura Kelly, raising the possibility that he might join the Trump administration in some capacity related to immigration or voting. He seemed to blow his opportunity to become Trump's immigration czar when he made ten demands, including 24/7 access to a government jet, walk-in privileges into the Oval Office, and a promise that the president would nominate him to be DHS secretary within six months if Kobach wanted the position.[67]

As the post-truth 2020 election season began, there was no indication that the Republican drumbeat of voter fraud might subside. Instead, more states passed new laws aimed at curtailing voter registration drives in the face of high African American turnout in recent elections. Armed with no more than an icicle, purveyors of the voter fraud myth, including President Trump, stood ready to undermine voter confidence in the election by simultaneously convincing Republicans that Democrats were trying to steal the election and convincing Democrats that Republicans were trying to do so.[68]

2

The Weakest Link

Two minutes late. "I just worked my ass off for nothing."

Joseph D'Alessandro, the director of elections planning for Broward County, Florida, was expressing his frustration. Three razor-thin elections in Florida—the 2018 contests for U.S. Senate between incumbent Democrat Bill Nelson and the outgoing Florida governor, Republican Rick Scott; for governor between Democrat Andrew Gillum and Republican Ron DeSantis; and for state agriculture commissioner—had come down to simultaneous statewide recounts. Scott led Nelson by only 0.14 percent of the vote after the initial counting of ballots, and Broward's election staffers had just spent days rushing against a state-imposed deadline to run more than seven hundred thousand ballots back through counting machines to find out if the totals they initially reported to state officials were accurate. And if the ballot counts statewide remained close after this machine recount, election officials were going to face another quick deadline for a hand recount of "undervotes," ballots that the machines had recorded as having no vote for an office, and "overvotes," ballots that the machines recorded as improperly having more than one vote for the same office.[1]

Under state law, the machine recount totals were due to the Florida secretary of state's office by 3 p.m. on November 15. Broward officials knew it was a tall task, but by working extended hours, they completed their recounts in all three close races by 1 a.m. the day of the deadline, leaving the rest of the day to determine voter preferences on 384 ballots that could not be read by the machines. Dr. Brenda Snipes, the supervisor of elections, announced that the county had finished the recounts on time and would submit the results to the state. Under the machine recount, Scott would have drawn 779 more votes than Nelson in the county than under the original count.[2]

But it didn't happen. Broward submitted its totals to the state at 3:02 p.m., two minutes past the deadline, and under state law those numbers could not be included in the totals. The frustrated D'Alessandro blamed the problem on "operator error" and unfamiliarity with the state's website. D'Alessandro's boss, Brenda Snipes, took responsibility but offered no apology. "An election like the one we just finished almost always has so many moving parts and so many components. . . . I'm pleased that we were able to accomplish what we did accomplish in the period of time that was available."[3]

Governor Scott and his supporters suggested that Snipes had deliberately sabotaged the submission of recount results because she supported Nelson. President Trump had started blaming Snipes for late vote totals in Broward County on November 9, even before all the snafus, telling reporters before boarding a presidential helicopter: "If you look at Broward County, they have had a horrible history. . . . And if you look at the person, in this case a woman, involved, she has had a horrible history." He added a somewhat incoherent comment suggesting that Democrats were trying to steal the election. "And Rick Scott who won by, it was close but he won by a comfortable margin, every couple hours it goes down a little bit. And then you see the people, and they were involved with the fraud of the fake dossier, the phony dossier, and I guess I hear they were somehow involved or worked with the GPS Fusion people, who have committed, I mean you look at what they've done, you look at the dishonesty, look, look, there's bad things gone on in Broward County, really bad things."[4]

Neither Scott nor Trump offered evidence of Snipes's bad intentions, and a state police investigation requested by Scott was abandoned when police received no credible allegations of malfeasance. The case seemed better explained by the Hanlon's Razor maxim: Don't attribute to malice what can be explained by incompetence.[5]

A retired educator and registered Democrat, Snipes was probably the most incompetent election administrator in a large jurisdiction in the United States. Republican governor Jeb Bush had appointed her to the position in 2003 after suspending her predecessor, Miriam Oliphant, for incompetence. And Snipes won reelection several times despite an abysmal track record.

In 2004, a year after taking office and only four years after the 2000 presidential contest had focused the nation's attention on Florida's troubled election system, Snipes's office failed to deliver fifty-eight thousand ballots to absentee voters who requested them. The Southern Christian Leadership Conference, an African American civil rights organization, called on Bush to suspend Snipes, saying she made the same mistakes that Bush had cited in suspending Oliphant. Snipes blamed the U.S. Postal Service, but there was no evidence it was at fault.[6]

In 2012, election workers discovered almost one thousand uncounted ballots in Broward County offices a week after the election. In 2016, Snipes's office left a voter initiative about medical marijuana completely off some Broward ballots. That same year, Broward officials violated state law by posting some election results on the county website before polls closed. Also in 2016, a court ruled that Snipes's office destroyed ballots after twelve months, in violation of a federal law requiring that they be preserved for twenty-two months.[7]

The 2018 election was probably Snipes's worst performance. In addition to Snipes's office missing the deadline for submission of the recount totals by two minutes, that machine recount ended up counting 2,040 fewer ballots than the original count. Following the required second (manual) recount, the Broward County canvassing board voted to submit final numbers to the state based on the Election Night totals rather than the totals from the machine recount. They did so because they feared that the recounted numbers were less accurate and the newer totals would disenfranchise more voters. The office admitted it had "mishandled" some ballots and commingled others in piles set aside for manual recounts. At least 180 ballots were tainted due to clerical error. Snipes had no good explanation for the discrepancies other than human error. "The votes are in the building. . . . I know that sounds trite, it sounds foolish." She said some staffers were "not as well trained as some others."[8]

Scott even had to sue Snipes in the middle of the counting process to find out the number of ballots that were still outstanding. This is the kind of information that election officials, in the interest of transparency and honesty, can and regularly do announce. Yet it took a public records lawsuit to get Snipes to do what was required by law.[9]

Then there was the design of the 2018 ballot itself. Florida had become infamous in 2000 for its badly designed ballots. There were the "hanging chads," little pieces of paper not completely dislodged from cardboard computer cards, first designed for voting by IBM in the 1960s using technology dating back to the 1890s. There was Palm Beach County's "butterfly ballot," with names of presidential candidates on both sides of the page pointing toward a place in the center for voters to punch out the chad for the candidate of choice. This led to many votes for two candidates or for the wrong candidate, including the famous "Jews for Buchanan"—elderly Jewish residents of

Palm Beach who mistakenly voted for Israel-basher Pat Buchanan when they thought they were voting for Al Gore. Less famous, but more significant in 2000, was Duvall County's experience. With thirteen presidential candidates running, Duvall listed the names of candidates on two separate pages and sent instructions telling voters to vote every page. About twenty-six thousand Duvall voters cast more than one vote for president in 2000, rendering those presidential ballots uncountable.[10]

In the 2018 U.S. Senate race, the ballot format problem in Broward County was undervotes, not overvotes. Gone were the hanging chads, but the new ballot placed the Senate race near the bottom left corner under the instructions of an ugly, crowded ballot. About 25,000 fewer votes were cast in the Senate race than in the governor's race, likely because of the poor design. Given that Broward was heavily Democratic, some worried it might have cost Nelson his Senate seat. The final official results had Scott beating Nelson by 10,033 votes out of more than 8 million cast. After the election, Florida amended its election law to prohibit the layout used in this race.[11]

Despite Snipes's terrible snafus over the years, Governor Scott suspended her from office for "misfeasance, incompetence, neglect of duty—or all of these" only after she botched the counting in his 2018 Senate race, and after she had already announced her resignation. After Scott suspended her, Snipes rescinded her resignation and sued him in federal court. She claimed the suspension violated her due process rights even though she had the right to a hearing before the state senate to contest her suspension. Snipes, who is African American, suggested to reporters that Scott's action was motivated by race. "'Jeb Bush did put me in this position, and that was following the removal of another black woman,' [she] told reporters, who [had] not ask[ed] about race or gender. Asked to explain more, Snipes said: 'I

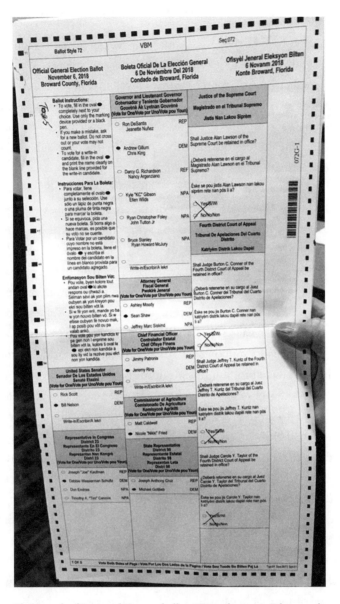

Photograph of Broward County ballot, November 2018 (Photo credit: David Smiley)

try to look at all factors, and it's sort of hard to rule out race. But I won't say, "Oh, I'm a black woman and that's why." I'm not saying that.'" The new governor, Ron DeSantis, made a deal to withdraw Snipes's suspension in exchange for her resignation. She resigned with, she said, her "name and. . . . dignity" intact.[12]

Partisanship. Incompetence. Failing election machinery. Elections decided by the slimmest of margins. Concerns about racial injustice. It seemed that Florida had not learned the right lessons from the 2000 election debacle, which ended with the U.S. Supreme Court deciding *Bush v. Gore*, terminating Democrat Al Gore's quest for a recount to wrest Florida's electoral votes and the presidency from Jeb's brother, Republican George W. Bush.

The story of the 2000 election is too long to tell here—I tell it in great detail in an earlier book, *The Voting Wars*—but a few words for those who are too young or too old to remember: the 2000 presidential election between Bush and Gore came down nationally to Florida's twenty-five Electoral College votes. On Election Night, Bush led Gore in Florida by 1,784 votes out of almost 6 million cast, a margin so tight that it triggered an automatic machine recount. Gore initially conceded, but then rescinded his concession once it was clear that the race was too close to call.[13]

The recounting process revealed a cluster of problems in how Florida's sixty-seven counties ran their elections: machinery and technological issues, including punch card voting machines that proved to be incredibly inaccurate in recording voters' preferences; legal issues, including unclear standards for when and how to conduct recounts; political issues, including the use of partisan election officials to set the rules covering deadlines, the counting of votes, and how voter intent should be determined on unclear ballots during recounts; and a host of equity issues, including a strict felon disenfranchisement law that fell heavily on Florida's African American population, and a shoddy voter purge system which was designed to keep felons off the rolls but which, by design or neglect, disenfranchised thousands of eligible voters with names similar to those of felons.

The dispute led to a host of lawsuits aimed at how election officials conducted the election, recount, and related legal proceedings. To many Democrats, the chief bad actor in 2000 was Katherine Harris, the elected Republican secretary of state, who served as the state's chief election officer and also as chair of Bush's election campaign in Florida. She not only ordered the racially discriminatory voter purge but also made a series of questionable decisions about how counties could conduct recounts and about the timing for various stages of protesting and contesting the election. All of these actions worked to benefit her fellow Republican. To many Republicans, the chief bad actor in 2000 was the Florida Supreme Court, dominated by Democrats, which overturned some of Harris's rulings and made controversial decisions that gave Gore additional chances to have votes recounted and included in vote totals.[14]

By the time *Bush v. Gore* arrived on the steps of the Supreme Court, recounts had cut Bush's lead down to 537 votes. With the deadline for Florida to certify its Electoral College votes looming, the Court's five conservatives held in an unsigned opinion that Florida's standards for conducting recounts violated the equal protection guarantees of the Constitution's Fourteenth Amendment. Rather than send the case back to the lower courts for counting using procedures that would comply with the Court's new equal protection standards, the Court said it was too late to count, given the Florida legislature's intent to fall within the "safe harbor" of a congressional statute guaranteeing that Congress would not challenge the state's Electoral College votes when submitted by a certain deadline.

In normal times, one would have expected the Court's liberal justices to be more interested in a muscular reading of the Equal Protection Clause than its conservative justices. But the conservatives united behind the nascent broad equal protection theory, even though Justice Antonin Scalia, who voted for it, reportedly thought the majority's reason was, "like we used to say in Brooklyn . . ., a piece of shit." The Court's four liberals divided on whether there were constitutional problems with how Florida conducted its recount. But they were united in their conclusion that Florida should have had a chance to conduct another recount under the Court's new standards. Yet the morning after the Court's decision, once it was clear the majority had made a revised recount impossible, Gore conceded.[15]

Florida 2000 gave the nation a wake-up call to doubt something it had largely taken for granted: that vote totals announced at the conclusion of American elections accurately reflected the voters' preferences. Over the next decade, the greatest improvements came in the area of voting technology: with the junking of punch card balloting technology and some other bad systems, places like Florida saw a 90 percent reduction in errors caused by machinery failing to count ballots as the voter intended. Congress helped spur the improvement by passing the Help America Vote Act of 2002 (HAVA), which, among other things, provided money for jurisdictions to replace aging machinery and established the United States Election Assistance Commission to certify good voting technology and take other steps to improve American elections. As attention has focused on the continuing problems in elections, many states have done much to shorten long lines and increase access to voter registration through adoption of online voter registration programs. In 2018, 84 percent of voters said they were "very" or "somewhat" confident that their vote was counted correctly.[16]

But many of the fundamental pathologies unearthed by the 2000 debacle have not changed even as new problems with voting technology have emerged, especially with the rising prospect of foreign hacking. Political actors realized that the courts were fertile grounds for fighting over election rules. American election litigation has nearly tripled since 2000, from an average of 94 cases per year before *Bush v. Gore* to an average of 270 cases after. Election litigation was up 23 percent in 2016 compared to 2012. The nonpresidential year of 2018 saw the most cases, 394, since at least since 1996 (and likely ever).[17]

Most important, the use of partisan election officials to decide key election questions remains a key feature across many of America's over ten thousand election jurisdictions. No state since 2000 moved from partisan to nonpartisan election administration, as is prevalent in other advanced democracies such as Canada and Australia. Instead, the Wisconsin legislature abandoned its nonpartisan system, which some considered the best election administration system of any state, after Republicans in the legislature said it was biased against their party.[18]

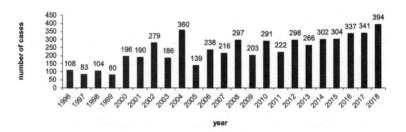

"Election challenge" litigation, 1996–2018 (Source: Author's compilation of data)

Florida took the secretary of state's office, which had been an elected position, and turned it into a gubernatorial appointment, arguably making the position even more partisan than it was under Katherine Harris. The change didn't improve the odds of a strong choice for the position. In early 2019, Florida secretary of state Michael Ertel resigned just three weeks after new governor Ron DeSantis appointed him to the job when a 2005 Halloween party picture surfaced. The picture showed Ertel, who is white, "in blackface and red lipstick, wearing earrings and a New Orleans Saints bandanna, and falsies under a purple T-shirt that had 'Katrina Victim' written on it." The party was only a few months after Hurricane Katrina devastated parts of Louisiana.[19]

Broward's experience in 2018 was not the only sign that Florida had taken insufficient steps to avoid election meltdown in the years since *Bush v. Gore*. Like Broward, Palm Beach County did not get its machine recount done on time in the Scott-Nelson Senate race or the two other close contests. The county claimed the machines it used to conduct the recount overheated. Palm Beach County supervisor of elections Susan Bucher told reporters that the ballot-counting machines "underwent maintenance right before the election," but "I don't think they were designed to work 24/7." Florida law had not contemplated that the state would have to undertake three simultaneous recounts under tight deadlines with inadequate machinery.[20]

Overall, Florida's record in 2018 was poor. Not including the 2,040 votes lost by Broward in its machine recount of votes, Florida counties collectively reported 3,000 fewer votes after the machine recounts than they reported on Election Day. "If I were a campaign, I'd be yelling and screaming," Charles Stewart III, director of the indispensable

Election Data and Science Lab at the Massachusetts Institute of Technology, told the *New York Times*. "I'd want a hand recount of every single ballot. . . . I don't see any evidence the wrong person was declared the winner. . . . But if four to five thousand votes didn't show up, you think, 'Hmm, I wonder if that's one of my ballots.' "[21]

While Palm Beach County election officials blamed the discrepancy in their county's vote totals on overheated machines, the machine manufacturer gave the *Times* a different explanation, saying that "its technicians had witnessed Palm Beach County elections workers, apparently worried that one of the machines was running too fast, jam a paper clip into the scanner's 'enter' button in an effort to slow it down. That, in turn, caused a short circuit that cut off the power." It is probably no surprise that Bucher resigned after Governor DeSantis suspended her in 2019 for a history of election administration problems.[22]

And then there was the case of Bay County, a community in the Florida Panhandle that was hit hard by Hurricane Michael a few weeks before the election. Governor Scott had signed emergency legislation allowing election officials in counties affected by the hurricane to extend the early voting period and to open more polling locations. But Mark Anderson, Bay County's supervisor of elections, did more than that: in clear violation of Florida law, he accepted 11 emailed ballots and 147 ballots sent in by fax. He told a reporter: "What would someone else do? The same cotton pickin' thing I did." Anderson's action recalled that of a 2000 Florida election official from another heavily Republican county, Clay County, who accepted two "overseas" ballots sent by fax from Maryland after the deadline for submission of ballots.[23]

In the 2018 elections, Bill Nelson sued Anderson to block faxed and emailed ballots from being counted, an effort he abandoned when he conceded the election to Rick Scott. At a December 2018 meeting of Florida election officials, Anderson received a standing ovation for his illegal action.[24]

Florida's election experience in 2018 reveals what I will term the Weakest Link Axiom of election administration: the accuracy of an election system, and voters' confidence in the system's fairness and accuracy during a contest close enough to go into overtime, is only as strong as the weakest parts of that system. It appears that most Florida election officials (like their equivalents around the country) acted competently and professionally in 2018, delivering the best service they could given the resources available to them. Isolated pockets like Broward County have larger problems. In an average election decided by a few percentage points or more, the average level of competence is enough to maintain voter confidence. The foibles get covered in the local press and occasionally gain national attention, there's a brief period of hand-wringing, and most people—aside from election professionals and academics—forget the problems until the next election season, when the press starts asking whether things have improved.

But when elections are very close, attention immediately focuses on the weakest link in the system. No one will care that most of Florida's sixty-seven counties counted their votes in a fair and timely way, without major foul-ups or violations of the law. Had the Scott-Nelson election been just a tiny bit closer and hung on recounts and court cases, the incompetence of the weakest links would have been the subject of popular obsession in a hyperpolarized and distrusting atmosphere.

What happened to those five thousand votes that went missing between the first and second recounts? Why didn't Broward use the new totals rather than the old ones? What was Brenda Snipes trying to hide in not allowing the public release of ballot totals? Did she deliberately sabotage the on-time submission of revised numbers because they helped Scott? Did the ballot-counting machines across Florida give different numbers between the original counts and machine recounts because they were hacked? What should be done about illegal ballots cast by fax or email in a heavily Republican county that were counted by a rogue election official who wanted to avoid disenfranchising his county's voters?

In the Trump era, even the normal ballot counting has become suspect in close elections when larger jurisdictions need days to count all of the valid absentee and provisional ballots. On November 12, 2018, just a few days after Election Day and while both the Florida U.S. Senate and governor's races remained too close to call, President Trump irresponsibly tweeted: "The Florida Election should be called in favor of Rick Scott and Ron DeSantis in that large numbers of new ballots showed up out of nowhere, and many ballots are missing or forged. An honest vote count is no longer possible – ballots massively infected. Must go with Election Night!"[25]

Never mind that "going with Election Night" would mean disenfranchising military and other overseas voters, whose ballots, according to many states' election laws, must still be counted even if they arrive after Election Night. The point was that Trump was calling the Florida vote count "massively infected" by criminal activity without any supporting evidence.

Race was an unspoken subtext of Trump's tweets and comments about Brenda Snipes. Trump has a history of attacking black women, such as calling his frequent critic Representative Maxine Waters "low

IQ," and his comments about Snipes came as he attacked six African American women in a three-day period. He often suggested, without evidence, that African Americans, immigrants, and other minorities who voted overwhelmingly Democratic were committing voter fraud and stealing elections.[26]

It is impossible to ignore how race plays into attacks on election administration in Democratic areas, and how pockets of incompetence like Snipes's Broward County are described by many on the right as intentional acts of fraud. It is a marked contrast with how the right treats incompetence by officials in Republican counties, such as that of Kathy Nicholas, the clerk in Waukesha County, Wisconsin. In a razor-thin state supreme court race in 2011, she initially misreported her county's numbers because she forgot some 14,315 votes she had stored on her laptop. When she remembered and reported those votes the day after the election, the statewide race flipped from Democratic to Republican. Incompetent officials in Republican counties are almost never accused of deliberate fraud.[27]

The election jurisdictions with the biggest problems tend to be those that include the largest cities, which are apt to have large Democratic majorities and often sizable minority populations. Jurisdictions with big cities also, not surprisingly, have the largest number of ballots cast. Even under the best conditions, they take the longest to count ballots. But cities also tend to have more poor and minority voters, who are much more likely to run into a problem, requiring them to cast provisional ballots that election officials must then process by hand. Democrats have also been increasingly reliant on absentee ballots, which take more processing time. As Professor Ned Foley, the reporter for the American Law Institute's nonpartisan project on election administration reform, explained in an important paper titled "A Big Blue Shift," these late-arriving, but perfectly legal, urban ballots tend to produce more Democratic votes, meaning that Republicans who lead on Election Day may see their leads shrink or evaporate as cities weigh in with late-counted votes. It is nothing nefarious, but it can look that way to people who do not understand the process, including former Speaker of the House Paul Ryan, who called the 2018 shift in California congressional seats from Republican leads to Democratic victories "bizarre."[28]

On top of that, large Democratic-leaning cities often get their election resources from Republican-leaning state legislatures. Democrats' common complaint is that legislatures give cities inadequate resources to run their elections. In 2004, for example, voters in Ohio cities with large African American populations, like Cleveland, had to wait in very long lines to vote, something Democrats blamed on the state's insufficient allocation of working voting machines to these areas. Many Democrats blamed these problems for John Kerry's loss to George W. Bush in the 2004 presidential election, which depended upon Ohio's Electoral College votes.[29]

Inadequately resourced cities tend to produce longer lines, in part because of resource allocation problems and inadequate training of poll workers. These problems sometimes lead to lawsuits to keep the polls open later, and some Republicans view court orders extending polling hours in minority-heavy cities as efforts by Democrats to gin up vote totals by bending the rules.

For example, in the close 2000 race for the U.S. Senate in Missouri between Republican John Ashcroft and Mel Carnahan (who died during the campaign and whose wife, Jean Carnahan, later served in his place), Senator Kit Bond threatened to ask federal investigators to examine "voter fraud" when a court ordered St. Louis polls to be kept open late after reports of an inadequate number of voting booths and equipment. Bond offered no evidence of such fraud.

Places such as St. Louis are hit with a double whammy: a poor voting experience followed by irresponsible fraud claims.[30]

This dynamic of big-city incompetence sold to the Republican base as voter fraud is bound to worsen unless election officials upgrade their voting technologies and staff training. In its final report, the Obama-appointed bipartisan Presidential Commission on Election Administration, headed by Bob Bauer and Ben Ginsberg, warned about an "impending crisis" of voting technology reaching the end of its useful life. Many jurisdictions in the United States replaced their voting machines after Congress provided funding in the 2002 Help America Vote Act, but now the replacement machines need replacing. The 2016 presidential election revealed that Michigan, particularly the large and largely African American city of Detroit, was one of the biggest problem areas.[31]

In the 2016 election, Donald Trump was able to put together a surprising Electoral College victory by narrowly winning three states that had previously trended Democratic in presidential races—Michigan, Pennsylvania, and Wisconsin. The total vote difference in the three states was roughly eighty thousand. The Clinton campaign calculated that there was no reason to request a recount because the margin, though close, was not so close that a recount was likely the change the results. But Green Party candidate Jill Stein, whom many Democrats blamed for siphoning votes away from Clinton and helping Trump, raised millions of dollars for recounts in these states. The call for recounts came after some on the left raised concerns that Russia could have hacked voting systems to change election results, even though there was no evidence such hacking actually took place. Some Trump and Clinton supporters believed Stein demanded the recount for her own purposes, such as to build up her mailing list for future solicitation, but the Clinton campaign participated in the recounts as observers.[32]

The recounts reached various points in the three states, and un-surprisingly, the results did not change. But in Michigan, where the final tally showed Trump beating Clinton by 10,704 votes out of approximately 4.8 million cast, the recount hit a snag in Detroit before courts called it off as unauthorized by state law. That snag revealed very disconcerting facts about the state of U.S. voting technology and inadequate training of election workers, and it led to a quick spread of conspiracy theories.[33]

Michigan requires each precinct to keep an electronic poll book listing voters' names and showing who voted. Under state law, votes from a precinct may be included in a recount only if the number of voters that the electronic poll book shows as having voted matches the number of votes tabulated by its corresponding optical scan voting machine. In Detroit, however, approximately 392 precincts had mismatched numbers. One of the worst examples, Precinct 152, recorded 306 people as having voted but had only 50 ballots in its sealed ballot box.[34]

These anomalies sparked claims from the right of widespread fraud. *World Net Daily*'s headline blared: "Stealing the Vote: Recount Uncovers Serious Fraud in Detroit." The story reported a ballot potentially being recast six times. *Fox News Insider* declared: "Oops! Stein's Recount Turns Up More Votes Than Voters in Detroit." The report included a link to a "Fox & Friends" video as well as a Fox & Friends tweet reading: "Jill Stein's crusade to expose voter fraud blows the lid off ballot box fraud in Detroit where Hillary Clinton won big." Even the sober *Detroit Free Press* had an inflammatory headline: "Detroit's Election Woes: 782 More Votes Than Voters."[35]

At first it was unclear just what went wrong in Detroit, but even at the beginning of the recount it appeared likely that a combination of machine failure, such as numerous instances of optical scan ballots jamming in the tabulation machines, and human error was the major culprit. A subsequent investigation by the Michigan Secretary of State's Board of Elections (BOE) placed the blame squarely on human error.[36] "BOE found no evidence of pervasive voter fraud or that widespread voting equipment failure led to the imbalances, yet the audit uncovered a multitude of human errors that prevented (or would have prevented) the presidential recount from proceeding in a significant number of precincts." Many of the problems stemmed from election workers not knowing how to properly record information in the electronic poll books, such as recording a spoiled ballot, or from the mishandling of provisional ballots. Many ballots were not properly put in the tabulation machines. BOE was able to reconcile the vote totals in almost half of the 392 unbalanced precincts by figuring out the election workers' errors on Election Night.[37]

The report continued: "In other instances, BOE determined that election workers left counted ballots in the tabulator bin at the end of the night instead of placing all ballots in a sealed container. The example of Precinct 152, widely cited in news media reports, is illustrative. When the sealed ballot container for this precinct was opened at the recount, it was found to contain only 50 ballots despite the fact that the poll book included the names of 306 voters. During the audit, BOE was able to confirm that all but one of the voted ballots had been left behind in the tabulator on Election Night. The audit refutes suspicions that the relatively small number of ballots placed in the ballot container could have been illegally tabulated again and again."[38]

Hanlon's Razor, again and again.

"AFTER FAILED HACKING ATTEMPT, SOS LAUNCHES INVESTIGATION INTO GEORGIA DEMOCRATIC PARTY." The weekend before the 2018 election, that all-caps headline greeted Georgia voters on the official website of the Georgia Secretary of State, the web page that Georgia voters visit to confirm their polling place, get information on candidates and ballot measures, and find out all things related to elections. The website was soon updated with another headline, "FAILED CYBERATTACK," and an official statement from the Secretary of State's office: "We opened an investigation into the Democratic Party of Georgia after receiving information from our legal team about failed efforts to breach the online voter registration system and My Voter Page." In fact, Democrats had done no hacking but had alerted election officials about possible vulnerabilities in the state's voter registration database.[39]

It was the most banana republic moment in the United States I could recall in two and a half decades of professionally following elections. Georgia's Republican secretary of state, Brian Kemp, was not only its chief elections officer but also the Republican nominee for governor. He was running against Stacey Abrams, a rising star in the Democratic Party. Abrams, an African American woman, made restoring voting rights a priority even before she ran for office. Kemp, who is white, was worried about the Abrams team's effort to get out the vote with absentee ballots. In audio from a speech leaked to *Rolling Stone* a few weeks before the election, he said that Democrats had submitted "an unprecedented number of" absentee ballot requests, "which is something that continues to concern us, especially if everybody uses and exercises their right to vote—which they absolutely can—and mail those ballots in, we gotta have heavy turnout to offset that." It was shocking to see a state's chief election officer, who was in charge of his own election, express worry that large numbers of people might vote in an upcoming election.[40]

If Brenda Snipes was perhaps the most incompetent county election official in the United States during the 2018 election season,

GO MOBILE
WITH THE NEW GA SOS APP!
App Store | Google play

GEORGIA
SECRETARY OF STATE
BRIAN P. KEMP

SECRETARY OF STATE | CORPORATIONS | ELECTIONS | LICENSING | SECURITIES | CHARITIES

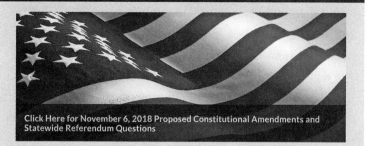

Click Here for November 6, 2018 Proposed Constitutional Amendments and
Statewide Referendum Questions

 NEWS AND ANNOUNCEMENTS

**SOS RELEASES MORE DETAILS OVER FAILED
CYBERATTACK, OFFICIALLY REQUESTS FBI TO
INVESTIGATE**
Posted: Sunday, November 04th 2018 in : General

ATLANTA – The Secretary of State's Office issues the
following update:"We opened an investigation into the
Democratic Party of Georgia after receiving information
from our legal team about failed efforts to breach the online
voter registration system and My Voter Page. We are
working with our private sector vendors and investigators
to ... [Read More]

**AFTER FAILED HACKING ATTEMPT, SOS LAUNCHES
INVESTIGATION INTO GEORGIA DEMOCRATIC PARTY**
Posted: Sunday, November 04th 2018 in : General

ATLANTA – After a failed attempt to hack the state's voter
registration system, the Secretary of State's office opened
an investigation into the Democratic Party of Georgia on the
evening of Saturday, November 3, 2018. Federal partners,
including the Department of Homeland Security and Federal
Bureau of Investigation, were immediately alerted."While
we cannot ... [Read More]

**CORPORATE
ANNUAL
REGISTRATION**
Click here to renew your
Annual Registration.

LICENSING
Click here to renew your
professional license
expiring on October 31,
2018.

SECURITIES
Click here to navigate to
the The Securities
Division of the Secretary
of State's Office.

ELECTION RESULTS
Click here to search the
results of the May 22
2018 Primary Election.

**INFORMATION
FOR PENDING
VOTERS**
Click here for
information that may

*Screenshot of the Georgia Secretary of State home page, November 4, 2018, the
Saturday before the November 2018 general election, as captured at https://
twitter.com/rickhasen/status/1059187255439372288*

Kemp was perhaps the most incompetent state chief elections officer, one who tried to hide his incompetence behind a lie aimed at giving him political advantage. Statewide chief elections officers do not run polling places, roll out the voting machines, or corral the volunteers, but they do other tasks that are essential to the smooth running of elections. Most important, they approve voting technology used across a state and maintain voter registration databases, which are used to determine who is eligible to vote in each election.

Kemp's tenure as Georgia's secretary of state had been rocky. He had been sued numerous times for choices he made concerning the statewide voter registration database. A number of the issues resurfaced during the 2018 elections. In one of his most important decisions, his office had put on hold about fifty-three thousand voter registrations because the names on the registration cards did not exactly match name information in the Department of Motor Vehicles database. A discrepancy as small as a missing hyphen in a name was enough to disenfranchise voters under Kemp's exact-match rules, which he tried to justify on antifraud grounds. Eventually a court required Kemp to allow those voters to vote at the polling place if they could produce identification that included a name that was a "substantial match" to state records. There was some confusion about these rules at some polling places. No doubt some eligible voters did not know this was an option and simply stayed home rather than try to vote.[41]

There were other problems too. Some new citizens were wrongly flagged as noncitizens and therefore denied registration because the state database was not up to date. Election officials throughout Georgia threw out absentee ballots for a lack of matching signatures on ballot envelopes without giving any notice to voters whose ballots were rejected, so that they could have a chance to prove their identity.

All of these issues were magnified because Kemp was running in a close, hyperpolarized, and racially charged election in a southern state whose demographics were starting to change to benefit the Democratic Party.[42]

It was hard to tell which of these actions were due to incompetence and which were attempted suppression. But probably nothing compared to Kemp's failures in maintaining the security of the state registration database and its electronic voting machines. Georgia remained one of the few states using electronic voting machines that do not produce a paper trail that would allow postelection audits to verify the electronic vote totals.

As we will see in the next chapter, in 2016, foreign actors associated with the Russian government attempted to infiltrate state voter registration databases and had some success, even changing data in Illinois (a change that was caught and corrected before the election). These hacking attempts prompted the Department of Homeland Security to designate the nation's voting systems as "critical infrastructure" and offer help to states in protect the systems from cyberhacking. Kemp was one of seven state officials to refuse DHS's help to assure the integrity of his state's database.[43]

Worse, while President Obama was still in office, Kemp accused DHS of attempting to "breach our firewall" and interfere with the state database. Homeland Security Secretary Jeh Johnson investigated and informed Kemp that "a worker at his agency's Federal Law Enforcement Training Center in Brunswick, Georgia, had merely verified the professional licenses of job applicants—'a service, as I understand it, your website provides to the general public.'" Kemp did not accept the findings and demanded that the new Trump administration look further into the charges. A later DHS Inspector General report confirmed what Johnson told Kemp: there was no hacking by

DHS, only a federal government employee accessing a public part of the Secretary of State site to verify someone's employment status. Kemp never retracted his accusation.

The *Atlanta Journal-Constitution* reported that at the time Kemp turned down DHS help in securing the voter registration database and gave a statement to *Politico* assuring the security of his state's voting system, "the computer servers that ran Georgia's election system were wide open to potential intruders. Voters' personal data, passwords that poll supervisors used on Election Day, the coding for memory cards with which voters cast ballots—all of it was readily accessible." These data security problems were long-standing. The *Journal-Constitution* reported that in 2015, Kemp's office "accidentally sent political organizations, media outlets and others a trove of confidential information about every Georgia voter. Kemp blamed a single employee, whom he fired." But the problems went much deeper.

Georgia had outsourced control and security of the state's voter registration database to Kennesaw State University, and long before the 2018 elections, cybersecurity researcher Logan Lamb had discovered holes in the school's security that would allow the addition, deletion, or changing of information. Lamb quietly brought the vulnerabilities to the attention of Kemp's office to give it a chance to patch things up, but the office did nothing until well after the information became public.

Meanwhile, activists concerned about the integrity of Georgia's electronic voting machines sued to block the state from using its election system during the 2018 elections. The concern was that these machines were subject to outside hacking and that without a paper trail, election results could not be independently confirmed.

Federal district court judge Amy Totenberg refused to issue a preliminary injunction preventing Georgia from using its insecure voting system in the 2018 elections, but only because there was too little time before the elections to make a change. She excoriated Kemp and his staff for "bury[ing] their heads in the sand" in the face of compelling evidence.

> This is particularly so in their dealing with the ramifications of the major data breach and vulnerability at the Center for Election Services, which contracted with the Secretary of State's Office, as well as the erasure of the Center's server database and a host of serious security vulnerabilities permitted by their outdated software and system operations. A wound or reasonably threatened wound to the integrity of a state's election system carries grave consequences beyond the results in any specific election, as it pierces citizens' confidence in the electoral system and the value of voting. Advanced persistent threats in this data-driven world and ordinary hacking are unfortunately here to stay. Defendants will fail to address that reality if they demean as paranoia the research-based findings of national cybersecurity engineers and experts in the field of elections.

She later barred the use of these voting machines after 2019.[44]

Then, just days before the 2018 election, a Georgia man named Richard Wright, who had a background in software management, went onto Georgia's voter registration website to confirm the accuracy of his voter registration information. According to the *Journal-Constitution*, Wright discovered two big flaws in the database. "First, downloading a sample ballot also 'allows you to download any file on the system.' . . . Second, he said, the web address for each individual's voter registration page included a unique numerical identifier, apparently assigned sequentially. Just by changing the digits, he wrote, 'you can download anyone's data and that includes a lot of . . . personally identifiable information, such as driver's license numbers or the last four digits of Social Security numbers.'"

Wright sent emails to organizations that were suing the state over their electronic voting machines and then to the Georgia Democratic Party's election protection team. Rachel Small, the volunteer who received Wright's email, forwarded it "to her supervisor, who in turn sent it to two computer security experts at Georgia Tech, all before noon Saturday. That appears to have been the extent of the Democrats' involvement."

Then, according to the *Journal-Constitution*, "One of the security experts from Tech . . . notified a national security agency (he declined to say which one) because he worried a hacker could manipulate Georgia's election. [The expert] shared Wright's findings with the FBI, then got in touch with attorneys representing the secretary of state in the voting-machine case."

Georgia election officials should have taken immediate emergency steps to plug vulnerabilities in the state's election system. They should have thanked Mr. Wright. Instead, in an unprecedented act of political chutzpah, Kemp took credible information indicating that his office had once again failed to provide adequate security to Georgia's voter registration database and turned it into an unwarranted and unsubstantiated political attack on Democrats, accusing them on the Secretary of State's official web page on the eve of a closely contested election of "cyberhacking" into the election, a state and federal crime. The office posted its press release shortly after it was contacted by a reporter from the website *WhoWhatWhy* to say it was about to post a story on the vulnerabilities Wright found.

The spokesperson for the Secretary of State's office suggested that Rachel Small was engaged in criminal activity. She texted reporters: "Who is Rachel Small? . . . Is that her real name, and for whom does she work? Why was she talking about trying to hack the secretary of state's system?" As the *Journal-Constitution* reported, Kemp's campaign released a statement around the same time "claiming that Democrats had attempted 'a fourth-quarter Hail Mary pass that was intercepted in the end zone.' 'These power-hungry radicals should be held accountable for their criminal behavior.'" Meanwhile, although denying it, the Secretary of State's office quietly made changes to patch the holes Wright had found.[45]

This episode featured some of the worst aspects of American elections: an incompetent chief election officer in charge of his own election used official state resources to make unwarranted accusations against his political opponents, all in an effort to deflect criticism that he was failing to do his job in assuring the integrity of his state's election system.

Georgia voters rewarded him by narrowly choosing him as governor over Stacey Abrams, 50.2 percent to 48.8 percent. Perhaps Kemp's efforts to keep the Democratic vote down had some effect on the election's outcome—we won't ever know. And as I argued in chapter 1, that is not the most important question. The most important question is why Kemp was able to make it harder for any eligible Georgia voter to vote and failed to take adequate measures to assure the integrity of Georgia's voting machines and voter registration database.

Rather than contest the election, Abrams's allies filed a new omnibus lawsuit claiming that under Kemp's management, the gross incompetence across the entire Georgia voting system violated the Constitution, the Voting Rights Act, and the Help America Vote Act. That case is currently pending, along with the separate lawsuit on Georgia's electronic voting system that Judge Totenberg is considering.[46]

Most American election administrators do a professional and often thankless job with inadequate resources, producing election returns in as competent and fair a way as they know how. Most voters are satisfied with the service they get from these hardworking public servants.

But then there are the weak links, like Brenda Snipes, the people in charge of Detroit's election system, and Brian Kemp. When elections are close enough to go to overtime, the news media and the interested parties seldom differentiate between incompetence and deliberate abuse—or they blur the line for partisan reasons. In these razor-thin elections, when the whole world is watching, the other administrators—the ones who have done their jobs fairly and well—may feel they have worked their asses off for nothing.

3

Dirty Tricks

The Russian trolls were meddling in American elections again. This time a swarm of Cyrillic-named Twitter bots were boosting controversial former Alabama supreme court justice Roy Moore in his 2017 race for the U.S. Senate. Or so it seemed.

Moore was running as a Republican against Democrat Doug Jones in a 2017 special election to fill the Senate seat that opened up when Jeff Sessions became Donald Trump's first attorney general. The Twitter operation seemed ham-handed. At least eleven hundred Russian-language accounts suddenly began following Moore on Twitter about eight weeks before the election, and journalists quickly took notice. The *Montgomery Advertiser* reported, "Many of the new followers for Moore appear to be bots, with only a handful of followers and generic profile art, including photos of singer Avril Lavigne. . . . The biographical descriptions of Russians following the former Alabama chief justice include at least one English statement from a profile that 'I love Russia,' but also include statements (rendered through Google Translate) such as 'I'm landing a sushi, I'm studying at the institute, I'm getting ready for my daughter's birth'; 'I live in Russia, from which the proud is sadly unipotent'; 'nice, paddling in all the souls of the company'; 'I sell axes, I sign a repost, the best man in the world'; 'ONE THOUGHT-THOUGHTS!' and 'Mongolia's first and only marketing magazine. Printed monthly.' "[1]

Moore's campaign was already struggling before the news reports of fake Russian supporters made people think of the Russian interference in 2016. He had twice been suspended as Alabama Supreme Court chief justice, first for refusing a federal court order to remove a large Ten Commandments statue he commissioned for display in the Alabama judicial building, and later for defying a U.S. Supreme Court decision recognizing the right of same-sex couples to marry. Despite running in solidly Republican Alabama, he would go on to lose the election to Jones after reports surfaced in the *Washington Post* of his attempted sexual encounter with a fourteen-year-old girl while he was a lawyer in his thirties.[2]

On the Russian followers, Moore's campaign released a statement claiming that "Doug Jones and Democrat operatives are pulling a political stunt on Twitter and alerting their friends in the media." The Jones campaign called Moore's accusation a "disgusting and pathetic lie," and added: "Maybe Moore should check with Vladimir Putin, who shares his views on depriving people of their civil rights."[3]

In fact, although Jones apparently had nothing to do with it and later called for an investigation, an independent political firm called American Engagement Technologies had been behind what they termed a "false flag" operation. The stated goal of the operation was to sway fifty thousand votes toward Jones by experimenting "with many of the tactics now understood to have influenced the 2016 elections." Fake Russian trolls were just a small part of the operation. According to portions of a leaked postelection report on what was dubbed "Project Birmingham," the group aimed to "radicalize Democrats, suppress unpersuadable Republicans ('hard Rs'), and faction moderate Republicans by advocating for write-in candidates. . . . We aggressively targeted evangelical hard Rs with messaging meant to provoke disgust and depress turnout."[4]

Executive Summary

In September - December 2017 ███████ ran a digital messaging operation to influence the outcome of the AL senate race In August, 2017, we developed a strategy of micro-targeting specific AL districts to radicalize Democrats, suppress unpersuadable Republicans ("hard R●"), and faction moderate Republicans by advocating for write-in candidates Our goal was to move 50,000 votes

We targeted 650 000 like AL voters, with a combination of persona accounts, astroturfing, automated social media amplification and targeted advertising Using these tools, we ran an aggressive campaign that contributed historically high turnout in the specific Democrat district we targeted a 5% drop in voter turnout compared to the 201   ngressional race in hard R distincts and drove write-in votes to a number of candi   ding one who unwittingly asked one of our conservative Facebook pages to en   1idacy (we obliged) There were 22,819 write-in votes, which, combined with a 30,   n Democrat turnout and a corresponding drop in hard R turnout, moved enough vot   a Doug Jones victory

Highlights:

- We performed rapid, repetitive, and sustain targeting of a select group of 650k likely AL voters on Facebook, resulting in 6 ?7m impressions to Alabamians over the course of the campaign (not counting additional organic reach of an estimated ◆ 5m)
- We targeted Democratic counties across AL with aggressive anti-Moore memes, and focused on Jones' history prosecuting the KKK This supported national GOTV efforts that drove historically high black voter turnout
- We targeted AL suburban, college-educated Republican women to persuade them not ● vote with their husbands According to Washington Post exit polling, "Jones made particularly large gains among white women", and "Most women and independents thought allegations against Moore are true"
- We established the ███████ Facebook page, which was authentic enough to voters that a write-in candidate reached out and asked for our endorsement
- We then strategically split the Republican vote by establishing a relationship with, and then supporting, that conservative write-in candidate
- We aggressively targeted evangelical hard Rs with messaging meant to provoke ● and depress turnout According to NY? exit poll analysis, turnout in hard R district down 5% from AL congressional elections in 2014, and ●5% from the 2016 presid● ●●ction●.

Leaked page from Project Birmingham, "After-Action Report"
(Source: Jeff Giesea)

Among the group's other activities was creating a Facebook page called Dry Alabama, which tried to tie Moore to fundamentalist Baptist groups advocating a ban on alcohol sales in the state. According to a *New York Times* story, the progressive activists behind the page "thought associating Mr. Moore with calls for a statewide alcohol ban would hurt him with moderate, business-oriented Republicans and assist the Democrat, Doug Jones."[5]

Jonathon Morgan, the organizer of another Facebook page, Alabama Conservative Politics, claimed that the page linked to credible news organizations such as the *Washington Post* and *Fox News*, and then used true information to persuade conservatives not to vote for Roy Moore. A separate effort used targeted digital ads to drive Democratic turnout up and Republican turnout down; organizers claimed they were able to "manufacture approximately 45k Twitter followers, 350k Retweets, 370k Tweet Favorites, 6k Facebook Comments, 10k Facebook reactions, 300k Imgur upvotes and 10k Reddit upvotes" to influence the election against Moore.

A write-in Senate candidate named Mac Watson reached out to Alabama Conservative Politics during the campaign and got the site's endorsement. After contacting the page's organizers, he gained ten thousand (likely fake) new Twitter followers and coverage in the *Washington Post*. Operatives also reported trying unsuccessfully to form a super PAC to boost Watson. An unwitting accomplice to Project Birmingham's efforts, Watson later said the support he received "was about the shifting of votes, to be honest with you."[6]

Much of Project Birmingham's efforts remain steeped in mystery. Reid Hoffman, the billionaire co-founder of LinkedIn, gave $750,000 to fund American Engagement Technologies, but he later apologized, claiming he did not know that AET would spread misinformation or engage in dirty tricks. Hoffman funded the project through a group called Investing in US, whose head, Dmitri Mehlhorn, eventually admitted that some of Project Birmingham's campaign efforts might have gone too far: "Some tactics, such as social media political advertising, are illegal for foreign entities but appropriate for U.S. citizens. That said, the whole point of our investment portfolio is to fight against the misinformation and group stereotypes so common among authoritarians here and abroad. For that reason, none of the portfolio we recommended should have engaged in group disparagement or scale misinformation. Such tactics may win a battle but lose the war, by giving up on the American ideal that we seek."[7]

Jonathon Morgan, of the cyber research firm New Knowledge, which had recently completed a report for the Senate Intelligence Committee on Russian interference in the 2016 elections, was outed as one of AET's contractors. Morgan admitted that New Knowledge started the Alabama Conservative Politics site and funded some Facebook ads, but he said it was an experiment about the role of social media in campaigns, and he vehemently denied being involved in other misinformation tactics or AET-funded activities. Facebook later closed his account for violating its terms of service.[8]

Tovo Labs, an AET-funded company, admitted running ads aimed at raising Democratic turnout and depressing Republican turnout, but it claimed it did so using only truthful information, not misinformation. Joohn Choe, of AET-funded Dialectica, admitted to targeting Christian women in Alabama via social media during the campaign to "encourage rejection of Roy Moore on religious grounds while emphasizing the pointlessness of voting pro-life and contrasting it with Alabama's scandalously bad" infant mortality rate. Choe didn't expressly admit to waging a disinformation campaign but said that eventually his "focus shifted from studying disinformation and opposing it experimentally to fighting it wholesale with whatever tools were at hand. Given the state of knowledge I had—that we have, as a society—I concluded that it was the only ethical option available at the time, and I believe it remains so." Activist Matt Osborne was less apologetic about spreading misinformation, calling his Dry Alabama campaign a "smashing success."[9]

Whether Project Birmingham moved many votes—let alone affected the outcome of the Moore-Jones race—cannot be known. It is
unlikely but possible. Out of about 1.3 million votes cast, Jones beat
Moore by 21,924, which is fewer than the 22,819 cast for write-in candidates, one of whom apparently was boosted by AET-funded activities. Hoffman's $750,000 in expenditures to AET were a small fraction
of the $49 million spent on the race. But who knows what finally
moved normally Republican voters to vote for Jones, vote for a write-
in, or stay home, and what may have gotten otherwise complacent
Alabama Democrats to the polls for Jones?[10]

Moore, unsurprisingly, blamed his loss on "systematic voter
fraud" but produced no evidence of it, leading even J. Christian Adams of the notorious Pence-Kobach voter fraud commission to call
the claims "very sad and humiliating." Moore would have been on
firmer ground if he had pointed to the social media disinformation
and propaganda activities of AET. During the special election, Alabama secretary of state John Merrill had complained to Twitter and
Facebook about efforts to manipulate the vote on both sides. "We
were asking for help," Merrill told the *New York Times*. "It was clear to
us that this was being done intentionally by certain parties to mislead
candidates and mislead candidates' supporters." But even if it had had
focused on disinformation efforts, Moore's campaign would have
been hard-pressed to prove that these activities were illegal. Alabama
attorney general Steve Marshall looked into the activities after the
AET story broke, but so far there have been no charges filed.[11]

Project Birmingham mirrored Russian tactics used during the 2016
presidential election in three significant ways: both featured social
media–fueled disinformation campaigns aimed at suppressing votes

against the supported candidate; both had an uncertain effect on election outcomes; and both involved at least some activities that were odious but legal.

In retrospect, Russian interference in the 2016 elections was both audacious and efficient, including a dirty tricks operation run out of St. Petersburg by Russia's "Internet Research Agency." The overall plan had three components: manipulation of public opinion via social media, which served as the model for AET's Project Birmingham; the hacking and releasing of embarrassing emails; and intrusion into state voter registration databases.[12]

Russia's Internet Research Agency (IRA) used a variety of social media platforms to foment American political unrest, including Facebook, YouTube, Twitter, Pinterest, and especially Instagram, which saw much more Russian activity than initial press reports suggested. Over 30 million users shared Internet Research Agency–created content on Facebook and Instagram between 2015 and 2017. In perhaps the most brazen example of Russian social media manipulation, in May 2016, as reported by NPR, "two groups of demonstrators faced off outside the Islamic Center in Houston Texas. On one side stood people drawn by a Facebook group called Heart of Texas. It had 250,000 followers. The group's tagline was folksy—homeland of guns, barbecue and your heart. They were there to demonstrate against the purported Islamization of Texas. On the other side were people who were also drawn by a Facebook group—United Muslims of America. It had 328,000 followers. Tagline—I'm a Muslim, and I'm proud. They were on the streets to save Islamic knowledge." Russian operatives established both Facebook groups for a grand total of $200.[13]

Special Counsel Robert Mueller's investigation into Russian interference in the 2016 election found "dozens of U.S. rallies organized by the IRA" in the run-up to the election, beginning with a "confederate rally" in November 2015.[14]

We likely will never know the full extent of Russian involvement in the 2016 elections or whether it affected election outcomes in close states such as Michigan, Pennsylvania, and Wisconsin. But the claim that Russian social media activity changed the election seems doubtful given the small scale of the Russian enterprise compared with the $6.5 billion spent by Americans.[15]

Here is what we know from U.S. government assessments and press reports about the social media manipulation. Russian agents ran social media campaigns trying to tilt the election in favor of Donald Trump, buying at least $100,000 in Facebook ads for that purpose. Mueller's investigation "identified numerous links between the Russian government and the Trump Campaign. Although the investigation established that the Russian government perceived it would benefit from a Trump presidency and worked to secure that outcome, and that the [Trump] Campaign expected it would benefit electorally from information stolen and released through Russian efforts, the investigation did not establish that members of the Trump Campaign conspired or coordinated with the Russian government in its election interference activities."[16]

The Russians, of course, were not the only ones using social media to influence votes. Campaigns, parties, and outside American groups did so as well. Trump campaign officials considered, but claim they ultimately rejected, offers to use Psy Group, a firm made up of former Israeli intelligence agents, for social media manipulation of Republican Party convention delegates and voters. Mueller examined a $2 million payment to Joel Zamel, Psy Group's head, from George Nader, who was working for the United Arab Emirates and had offered help to the Trump campaign. Nader claimed the $2 million payment was connected to help given by Psy Group to the Trump campaign. Erik Prince, former head of Blackwater, who was under investigation by the special counsel, arranged one of the meetings that brought Psy Group's proposals to the Trump campaign's attention. Psy Group later closed down under intense media (and perhaps law enforcement) scrutiny, but not before it unsuccessfully tried in 2017 to manipulate results in an obscure hospital district recall election in Tulare, California. The parts of Mueller's final report that were public as I wrote this included no reference to Psy Group, or to Prince's or Nader's involvement with it. It may be the subject of an investigation referred to the FBI or another part of the Justice Department at the close of Mueller's investigation.[17]

As to Russian involvement, a joint report issued in January 2017 by the Central Intelligence Agency, the Federal Bureau of Investigation, and the National Security Agency confirmed Russian attempts to influence the outcome of the 2016 elections, create instability, and favor Trump over Democratic candidate Hillary Clinton: "We assess Russian President Vladimir Putin ordered an influence campaign in 2016 aimed at the US presidential election. Russia's goals were to undermine public faith in the US democratic process, denigrate Secretary Clinton, and harm her electability and potential presidency. We further assess Putin and the Russian Government developed a clear preference for President-elect Trump. We have high confidence in these judgments."[18]

Russia's extensive propaganda effort involved more than publishing negative stories about Clinton and U.S. interests. It also spread "fake news," false stories aimed at damaging Clinton and helping Trump. "For example, [Russian news website] Sputnik published an article that said the [John] Podesta email dump included certain incriminating comments about the Benghazi scandal, an allegation that turned out to be incorrect. Trump himself repeated this false story" at a campaign rally. Russia used some of that $100,000 Facebook ad purchase to spread false reports to specific populations, including aiming certain false reports at journalists who might be expected to spread the misinformation.[19]

What stood out more than anything else in the Internet Research Agency's social media efforts was Russia's primary focus. The 2013 North Carolina Republican voter suppression law had "targeted African-American voters with almost surgical precision," and so did the Russians. Although they did much to foment social media unrest in general by highlighting divisive issues such as immigration, foreign affairs, and gay rights, they devoted a disproportionate share of resources toward convincing African Americans to stay home and not vote for Hillary Clinton. As a December 2018 report by New Knowledge explained, "While other distinct ethnic and religious groups were the focus of one or two Facebook Pages or Instagram accounts, the Black community was targeted extensively with dozens." On YouTube, for example, "By far the most content was related to Black Lives Matter & police brutality: 1063 videos split across 10 different channels (59% of the channels, 96% of the content)." The Internet Research Agency used not just bots but also humans, who took on American personas to make direct contact with activists in the United States. It created an ecosystem around the "Black Matters" brand (a name suspiciously similar to the unrelated Black Lives Matter movement), curating linked accounts to ensure that African American readers trusted the site and heard its messages repeated across multiple sites.[20]

A report by Oxford University researchers for the Senate Intelligence Committee found that "messaging to African Americans sought to divert their political energy away from established political institutions by preying on anger with structural inequalities faced by African

Americans, including police violence, poverty, and disproportionate levels of incarceration. These campaigns pushed a message that the best way to advance the cause of the African American community was to boycott the election." For example, "Attacks on Clinton and calls for voter disengagement were particularly clear [on an IRA Facebook page called] Blacktivist during September, October, and November 2016, with statements such as 'NO LIVES MATTER TO HILLARY CLINTON. ONLY VOTES MATTER TO HILLARY CLINTON' (Blacktivist, 29 October 2016), another one argu[ing] that black people should vote for Jill Stein (Blacktivist, 7 October 2016), or not vote at all, with the claim: 'NOT VOTING is a way to exercise our rights' (Blacktivist, 3 November 2016)." According to *NBC News,* as late as 2018, Russian operatives who had participated in the 2016 election interference looked for new ways to foment racial discord, "including a suggestion to recruit African-Americans and transport them to camps in Africa 'for combat prep and training in sabotage.' Those recruits would then be sent back to America to foment violence and work to establish a pan-African state in the Southern U.S., including South Carolina, Georgia, Alabama, Mississippi and Louisiana."[21]

Russia's IRA also disseminated "voter fraud" memes aimed at right-wing groups, suggesting that minorities would use voter fraud to try to steal the election for Clinton. The most-shared IRA-sourced Facebook post mentioning Hillary Clinton during the election season showed a picture of a group of Latinos, waiting in a long line, with the meme, "Like if you agree only U.S. citizens should be allowed to vote." (The picture was lifted from a 2012 AP photo entitled *California Hispanics* of "people living in the U.S. without legal permission wait[ing] outside the Coalition for Humane Immigrant Rights in Los Angeles.") According to New Knowledge, "There were 109 posts devoted to creating and amplifying fears of voter fraud; the overwhelming majority

Example of Russian disinformation meme, 2016
elections (Source: New Knowledge report)

of them targeted right-wing audiences. 71 were created in the month leading up to election day, and made claims that certain states were helping Sec. Clinton win, that militia groups were going to polling places to stop fraud (called for volunteers to participate), that civil war was preferable to an unfair election or the election of Sec. Clinton, that 'illegals' were overrepresented in voter rolls in Texas and elsewhere, or were voting multiple times with Democratic Party assistance. . . . The prevalence of this narrative suggests they may not have expected Trump to win; regardless, they intended to incite violence if he did not."[22]

Very little of this Russian social media activity appears to have been illegal under federal election law. Although federal campaign finance law bars foreign governments, entities, and individuals from

Example of Russian meme on alleged noncitizen voting, 2016 elections (Source: New Knowledge report; original source of photograph: Associated Press/Damian Dovarganes [2012])

making expenditures in connection with federal elections, the law might cover only the tiny sliver of IRA activity that involved paid ads calling expressly for the election or defeat of a federal candidate, such as the Russian-paid ad stating, "Vote Republican, vote Trump, and support the Second Amendment!" Much of what the IRA did involved no paid ads at all. Further, many of the paid social media posts, such as one that read, "Hillary is a Satan, and her crimes and lies had proved just how evil she is," would not be illegal campaign ads, at least under the interpretation of the foreign spending ban that Justice Brett Kavanaugh wrote in 2012 when he served on the United States Court of Appeals, because they did not expressly urge a candidate's election or defeat. When Mueller indicted the IRA and thirteen Russian nationals working for it, he did not directly charge campaign finance violations; instead he charged them with fraud, deceit, and identity theft. We will probably never know if federal prosecutors would be able to prove most of those claims, because the people charged with those crimes are unlikely ever to end up in U.S. custody.[23]

Perhaps more important, the Russian social media campaign provided the blueprint for social media manipulation by Project Birmingham. Domestic groups engaging in Russia-type manipulation likely would not be breaking any campaign finance laws as long as they are not candidates, political parties, or registered political committees that have to report all campaign-related expenditures; they avoid any words of express advocacy of the election or defeat of candidates; and they don't feature candidates in certain television and radio ads broadcast close to the election.

Whether domestic groups engaging in misinformation campaigns could be charged with fraud or deceit for lying about facts or their identity on social media is uncertain, especially since the courts have given people broad First Amendment protection to lie in campaigns so long as they steer clear of defamation. Congress could try to pass new laws in this area, such as those that would improve disclosure of the sources of online ads, but so far, Republicans in Congress have shown no interest in doing so. In any case, many of the messages sent by foreign and domestic sources in 2016 were not false but contained opinions calculated to incite voters' negative partisanship, fear, and distrust.

Meanwhile, campaigns themselves are becoming more adept at "hypertargeting" voters with true, false, or manipulated messages. Former Facebook chief security officer Alex Stamos told *Yahoo Finance*,

> People are writing books right now about whether the overall Russian activity affected the election. . . . We might never

know. Quantitatively, the direct Russian activity is still quite small. Even with everything we know now. . . . Almost certainly the thing on Facebook that was most impactful in the election was the fact that the Trump campaign and the Republican PACs were so much better at Facebook ads than the Democratic side. You're talking about well over 100 times more dollars spent than the Russians did, and not quite twice what the Democrats did. . . . The Russian stuff was not that advanced . . . the Trump campaign was generating thousands of ads programmatically. They were testing those ads against hundreds of different segments of the population. They were automatically, then, saying, this one tested well, we'll put our money behind it.[24]

As Professor Nate Persily put it, "In the context of political advertising and election campaigns, we worry about the unfair advantage in the attainment of political power that goes to the best manipulator with the best data. . . . As microtargeting has become increasingly sophisticated, people lose confidence in the marketplace of ideas as the test for democracy-relevant truths."[25]

Work by political scientist Brendan Nyhan and others shows that worries about the effects on voter choice of deliberately false information spread via social media so far have been exaggerated. But Nyhan is concerned that pervasive discussions about fake news can lower voter confidence in legitimate news. Further, misinformation concerns are only bound to get worse as technology improves a user's ability to create false images and documents. The latest worry is "deep fakes," which are manipulated audio and video clips that can make a politician or celebrity appear to say or do anything the manipulator wants. As these images proliferate, voters will literally not be able to believe what they see on the screen. To make matters worse, we can expect what law professors Bobby Chesney and Danielle Citron call the "liar's dividend": "deep fakes mak[ing] it easier for liars to avoid accountability for things that are in fact true." Just think of Donald Trump's cries of "fake news" in response to anything that reflects negatively on him. With so many fake images and documents floating around, it will be very easy for candidates to deny they said or did what the image or video shows. As a headline in the tech magazine *Motherboard* put it, in an article about the ability to superimpose the head of any celebrity onto an actor's body in a porn video, "We Are Truly Fucked."[26]

The Russian 2016 strategy was less to spread false information than to exploit existing schisms in American society. The fuel was American polarization and hatred. The Russians just had to light the match. Those schisms are not going away, even as technology for manipulation improves with each election. As election law scholar Justin Levitt put it at a January 2019 forum on voting rights, the Russians "hacked us, rather than hacking the technology." Now we are perfectly capable of hacking ourselves.[27]

The two other forms of Russian interference in the 2016 elections, leaking of stolen emails from Democratic National Committee and Clinton campaign officials, and attempts to break into voter registration databases, are more clearly illegal and just as dangerous. The DNC emails revealed embarrassing facts about the party and the Clinton campaign strategy. Specific emails about the party's poor treatment of Clinton competitor Senator Bernie Sanders during the Democratic primary season forced Representative Debbie Wasserman-Schultz to resign as the DNC chair. The revelations were dripped out over a period of months by WikiLeaks, D.C. Leaks, and a hacker associated with the Russian government under the name Guccifer 2.0.[28]

Trump adviser Roger Stone admitted contact with the person tweeting as Guccifer 2.0 as well as (through an intermediary) with Julian Assange of WikiLeaks. "In August [2016]," the *New York Times*'s Matthew Rosenberg and Maggie Haberman reported, "Mr. Stone wrote on Twitter that John D. Podesta, Hillary Clinton's campaign chairman, would soon go through his 'time in the barrel.' Weeks later, WikiLeaks began publishing a trove of Mr. Podesta's hacked emails, the daily release of which was seen as damaging to the campaign." In 2019, Mueller indicted Stone for, among other things, lying about his 2016 contacts with WikiLeaks.[29]

Facebook's Alex Stamos explained how Russian security forces adeptly spread the leaked information. "So once they got this stuff in the hands of Politico and The Hill and others . . . those guys wrote the first stories, and then The New York Times, Washington Post, and others amplified it, and with 24-hour cable news, whether we took down their Facebook accounts or not didn't matter." Stamos tweeted in November 2018, "The mass media was completely played by the [Russian security services] and wrote the stories they wanted after the DNC and Podesta disclosures. You could argue that this was much more impactful than the IRA disinfo, and there has been almost no self-reflection by NYT/WaPo/WSJ/TV on their role."[30]

As to the infiltration of state voter registration databases, the best information we have is that the attempted cyberattacks were widespread, with one report claiming that the hacking hit systems in thirty-nine states, and the government confirming attacks in twenty-one. The Mueller report noted, "In one instance in approximately June 2016, [Russian government agents] compromised the computer network of the Illinois State Board of Elections by exploiting a vulnerability in the

SBOE's website. The[y] then gained access to a database containing information on millions of registered Illinois voters, and extracted data related to thousands of U.S. voters before the malicious activity was identified." Two Florida counties also saw their registration databases hacked, but the FBI would not reveal their names. The *Washington Post* reported one was a small county in the Florida Panhandle, Washington County.[31]

The level of attacks was so high that Obama administration officials used the "red phone" to warn Moscow to stop. After the Department of Homeland Security got involved, "thirty-seven states reported finding traces of the hackers in various systems. . . . In two others—Florida and California—those traces were found in systems run by a private contractor managing critical election systems." U.S. senator Marco Rubio confirmed that hackers were in a position to alter information on an unnamed Florida county's voting rolls. Rubio told the *New York Times* in 2019 that his "biggest concern is that on Election Day you go vote and have mass confusion because voter registration information has been deleted from the systems." So far as we know, the Russian efforts may have undermined voter confidence in 2016, but they did not alter any votes stored on government computers or devices.[32]

DHS efforts to fend off new attacks on voter registration databases and voting machine software will eliminate some existing vulnerabilities, but there is little reason to believe those efforts will succeed perfectly. Hardware and software are never static, and technology updates provide new opportunities to find and exploit vulnerabilities. Although decentralization of election databases in each state might seem beneficial because an attack on one state's database does not necessarily affect voting in other states, decentralization and the variety of computer systems multiply the significant challenge of defending against attacks.

Attacks on voter databases or voting machines can undermine voter confidence in the integrity of the vote even if successfully thwarted. And there will likely still be bonehead officials such as Georgia's former secretary of state (and current governor) Brian Kemp, who refused DHS help and instead accused the department of trying to hack into Georgia's voter registration database. Voters still sometimes have to sue to get election officials to take steps to ensure the integrity of voting systems.[33]

As for the hacking of emails, it has become relatively easy for hackers to find vulnerabilities in email systems, often through phishing tricks aimed at getting people to voluntarily turn over their passwords. This weakness has led some politicians to take new defensive measures, especially as the hackers have now included false documents within a larger batch of genuine ones. Emmanuel Macron's campaign partially thwarted a Russian hack of documents related to the 2017 French presidential election when the campaign "planted their own false documents throughout their own system to create a smokescreen of distrust." Not all campaigns will be as sophisticated as Macron's, and next time the Russians (or others) might do a better job of faking their documents and timing their release.[34]

If the Russians or other foreign governments really wanted to use hacking to disrupt an American presidential election, the most direct and dangerous way would be to bring down the electrical grid on Election Day in a swing-state Democratic city such as Milwaukee or Detroit. There's good reason to believe they already have the capability to do so.

A January 2019 *Wall Street Journal* article, "America's Electric Grid Has a Vulnerable Back Door—And Russia Walked through It," makes for terrifying reading. Like the DNC hacks, the Russian hacks into systems that control American infrastructure such as power grids and dams began with phishing exercises and planting malware aimed at gaining access to critical computer networks. For example, Russian agents apparently targeted a small private publisher of trade journals named *Consulting-Specifying Engineer* and *Control Engineering* by planting lines of code on the journals' websites that uploaded malware when system engineers visited the sites.[35]

Hackers also directed phishing emails to contractors and subcontractors of major electrical utilities, working their way up the supply chain with passwords that employees were tricked into turning over. For example, business associates of Mike Vitello, an employee at a fifteen-person Oregon firm working with utilities and public agencies, received a fake email with an attachment purportedly from Vitello. When recipients tried to download the attachment, a message directed some of them to a forged Dropbox log-in page, where Dropbox credentials could be stolen. "Once Mr. Vitello realized his email had been hijacked, he tried to warn his contacts not to open any email attachments from him. The hackers blocked the message." The *Journal* article concluded with the cybersecurity experts' understanding that "Russian government hackers likely remain inside some systems, undetected and awaiting further orders."[36]

For proof of the viability of disrupting an American city's electrical grid on Election Day, we need look no further than the repeated successful attacks begun in 2015 by the Russian government on Ukraine's electrical grid, which led to a series of electrical outages. According to an extensive report in *Wired*, the attacks on Ukraine's power systems, using malware called "BlackEnergy," began with "a phishing email impersonating a message from the Ukrainian parliament. A malicious Word attachment had silently run a script on the victims' machines, planting the BlackEnergy infection. From that foothold, it appeared, the hackers had spread through the power companies' networks and eventually compromised a [virtual private network] the companies had used for remote access to their network—including the highly specialized industrial control software that gives operators remote command over equipment like circuit breakers."[37]

The most serious attack, in December 2015, shut down power in three areas of Ukraine for an hour. Had it lasted much longer, pipes could have begun freezing as water pumps stopped working. The attack was more sophisticated than the original BlackEnergy infection. Hackers took over the computers at one power plant using tools that the plant's IT department had set up to assist employees with computer problems, "bricked" (rendered permanently inoperable) devices that allowed plant operators to digitally control key circuit breakers, and even disabled the battery backups to deal with power outages in the power plants themselves. "With utmost precision, the hackers had engineered a blackout within a blackout."[38]

American election law is a patchwork of federal, state, and local laws, many of which are inadequate to deal with natural and man-made emergencies on Election Day. After the September 11, 2001, attacks on the World Trade Center (which was an election day in New York City) and a series of debilitating hurricanes in Florida and Louisiana, election scholars have sought to have states come up with rules for dealing with terrorist attacks and disasters on Election Day.[39]

But most do not have adequate plans or legal rules in place for dealing with disasters, and U.S. presidential elections present an especially difficult challenge because of our uniform national Election Day. As political scientist Norm Ornstein wrote in 2018, "We have no Plan B to take the impact into account if a national election is disrupted. There are no do-overs and no mechanism in place to ameliorate the effect."[40]

If voters in all states other than Wisconsin or Michigan were able to vote on Election Day, and only parts of Democratic cities like Milwaukee or Detroit were hit with deliberate blackouts, leaving white, rural Republican voters in the majority, would courts order a revote? Would the revote apply to those cities only, to the states, or to the nation as a whole? Would a city like Detroit, with a history of election mismanagement, be up to the task of rerunning a presidential election under such stressful conditions? Would a court order of a partial revote provoke a constitutional crisis, if the presidential candidate who was ahead (or the candidate's party in Congress) refused to abide by the results of the revote? Would Russian and other agitators spread false information about whether the revote had been properly run?

High-tech dirty tricks, which can involve both illegal and legal methods of disrupting the voting process or manipulating public opinion, threaten to undermine America's faith in the fairness and accuracy of the election process, even if they do not directly alter election outcomes and even if (maybe especially if) the efforts are detected before all voters have cast their ballots. But not all dirty tricks require sophisticated hackers operating out of black sites.

Consider the actions of Leslie McCrae Dowless Jr., a political operative working around the poor rural area of Bladen County, population 33,478, in southeastern North Carolina. For years, Dowless had been running remarkably successful absentee ballot operations for both Democratic and Republican campaigns. In 2016, for example, in an otherwise close contest, 98 percent of absentee ballots in Bladen County in the Republican primary for North Carolina's Ninth Congressional District went to his client Robert Pittenger, who won the primary and then the general election.[41]

In 2018, Mark Harris, who had lost to Pittenger in that primary by 134 votes, ran against him again. This time Harris hired Dowless. He later claimed he did not know that Dowless had previous felony convictions for insurance fraud and perjury. Dowless ran absentee ballot operations for Harris, who beat Pittenger in the Republican primary and then beat his Democratic challenger Dan McCready by 905 votes in the general congressional election.[42]

North Carolina's state board of elections, surprisingly, refused to certify the results, citing evidence of potential criminal activity by Dowless and his accomplices that were connected to his absentee ballot operations. Absentee ballot fraud, while rare, is much more likely than voter impersonation fraud at a polling place, especially in areas like Bladen County that lack major independent media, because absentee ballots can be bought, stolen, altered, or destroyed outside the presence of election officials.

But eventually word got out, and investigators accused Dowless of a number of questionable activities. He had allegedly instructed his workers to collect absentee ballots from voters, including blank absentee ballots, in violation of state law prohibitions on so-called ballot harvesting; held as many as eight hundred absentee ballots rather than turn them in to election officials; stolen some absentee ballots; and perhaps completed some ballots that voters did not fully complete. Whatever Dowless did, it worked for Harris: according to a *New York Times* analysis, "In Bladen County this year, Mr. Harris won 61 percent of the accepted absentee ballots, even though registered Republicans accounted for only 19 percent of the ballots submitted."[43]

The *Times* interviewed Jeneva Legions, a thirty-year-old voter whom an apparent Dowless operative persuaded to turn over her unsealed, signed absentee ballot. "I thought she worked for the county. I thought she was one of the voting people coming to get my ballot."

Buzzfeed News reported that some of Dowless's workers, who were paid cash for their campaign work, stole ballots from elderly African American voters and used Dowless's cash to buy opioids. Jessica Dowless, one of Dowless's part-time workers (and the wife of a distant Dowless relative), said another worker in his office "was so fucking high the other day she passed out at the fucking computer." She added, "One of the workers who collected absentee ballots from residents was a 'pill head.'"[44]

The apparent shadiness of Dowless's operation had been known for some time in Bladen County. In January 2018, state election officials asked the Justice Department and Robert Higdon, the Trump-appointed U.S. attorney for the Eastern District of North Carolina, to investigate Dowless and the problems with absentee ballots in the 2016 elections. According to a *Washington Post* report, state officials followed up the next day with an eight-page memorandum describing potential illegality. Josh Lawson, general counsel for the state elections board, told the *Post* that these efforts "did not result in prosecutions or substantial work in the district before the election." Marshall Tutor, a retired North Carolina elections board investigator who investigated the 2016 elections in Bladen County, expressed his frustration to the *Post*: "You dig and dig and dig, and then nothing comes of it, which is quite frustrating."[45]

Rather than address the very strong evidence of election fraud in Bladen County, Higdon directed his office to focus instead on the apparently much smaller problem of noncitizen voting, at one point issuing unprecedented subpoenas for voting records from across North Carolina just as election officials were preparing to run the 2018 elections. Tutor told the *Post* that Higdon's "office is extremely interested in noncitizens who vote and made a huge deal out of that and subpoenaed all kinds of documents, but he has no interest in this other matter? It's cherry-picking."[46]

Why the skewed priorities? A former assistant U.S. attorney who worked for him told the *Post* that Higdon took his marching orders from Washington, and that Attorney General Jeff Sessions had pushed for a focus on crimes committed by immigrants. "He would always say by name, 'President Trump and Attorney General Sessions have directed that we do X, Y and Z, and we're going to do that' . . . 'And he would note that during meetings—how things are going to change in the office.' "[47]

So far, Higdon's efforts against noncitizen voting have had underwhelming results. In February 2019, a sixty-six-year-old grandmother named Denslo Allen Paige pleaded guilty in federal court to helping her boyfriend, Guadalupe Espinosa-Pena, a permanent legal resident, register to vote. Paige told *HuffPost* that Espinosa had talked a lot about politics, and she was not sure whether or not he was eligible to vote as a legal alien, even though she had worked as a poll worker in the past. They filled out the voter registration form without checking the box indicating that Espinosa was a citizen, expecting someone would let them know if he was not eligible.

The assistant U.S. attorney prosecuting the case told the court at sentencing that Paige and Espinosa went to "a help desk where there is a person who processes the voter registrations." Paige "admitted that she brought her boyfriend, Espinosa, she knew that he was not a U.S. citizen, and they left the box to the question, 'Are you a U.S. citizen?' blank. So it was blank as to 'Yes'; it was blank as to 'No.' And she stated that they even had a green card for Mr. Espinosa present. And my understanding was that the help desk person saw that; and nonetheless, the form was taken, processed, and Mr. Espinosa was registered to vote. And he, in fact, voted." An unknown person later checked the citizenship box after Espinoza and Paige turned it in. A court sentenced Paige, who works at Walmart, to two months in prison and a $250 fine; she faced up to five years in prison and $250,000 in fines.[48]

At the very least, Paige should have known better than to try to register her noncitizen boyfriend; the voting form itself indicated that a person should stop filling out the form if he or she is not a citizen. The sentence she received seemed appropriate for her conduct.

On the scale of dirty tricks, Paige's action was inconsequential. She affected at most one vote. But her plea gave Higdon's office a chance to issue a press release that greatly exaggerated Paige's former role as a volunteer poll worker: "Former North Carolina Board of Elections Election Official Sentenced to Prison for Aiding and Abetting Voting by an Alien in the 2016 General Election." Calling her a "Board of Elections Election Official" and failing to mention that she was trying to register her boyfriend was misleading at best, and the press release made it sound as if Higdon's office was doing much more than it was to combat noncitizen voting.[49]

So far, although North Carolina has indicted Dowless for a number of ballot-related crimes, Higdon's office only belatedly investigated Dowless. Federal authorities have shown at best a warped sense of priorities and revealed that the Trump administration's purported focus on rooting out major voter fraud was not serious.[50]

Let's hope other parts of the Trump administration are more serious about rooting out cyberthreats to America's power grid, critical infrastructure, and voting technology, and that they take defensive measures despite being led by a man who has proved himself more than willing to look the other way (at best) regarding Russian involvement in American elections, particularly when that involvement benefits him. The New York Times reported in April 2019 that President Trump's chief of staff, Mick Mulvaney, told then DHS secretary Kirstjen Neilsen not to bring up the topic of possible Russian interference in the 2020 election in front of the president. In a 2019 meeting, Mulvaney "made it clear that Mr. Trump still equated any public discussion of malign Russian election activity with questions about the legitimacy of his victory. According to one senior administration official, Mr. Mulvaney said it 'wasn't a great subject and should be kept below his level.' "[51]

4

"Stolen"

"So this year, we have an election coming up on November 8th. So important that you get out and vote. So important that you watch other communities, because we don't want this election stolen from us. We don't want this election stolen from us. We do not want this election stolen."[1]

Donald Trump was speaking to an enthusiastic crowd in Ambridge, Pennsylvania, a town of under eight thousand people outside of Pittsburgh, repeating three times his warning of a stolen election. The rally was in October 2016, the day after Trump's second debate against his Democratic opponent Hillary Clinton. He was slipping in the polls, and he was warning his mostly white audiences about the supposed dangers of voter fraud coming from "other communities."[2]

That evening, at a rally in Wilkes-Barre, Pennsylvania, Trump was more explicit about those "other communities": "Honestly, folks, you know I went to school in Philadelphia and I love Philadelphia. I love Philadelphia and I hope we're going to do great in Philadelphia. I went to school there. I love the school. I loved everything but I just hear such reports about Philadelphia. And we have to make sure we're protected. We have to make sure the people of Philadelphia are protected that the vote counts are 100 percent. Everybody wants that, but I hear these horror shows. I hear these horror shows and we have to make sure that this election is not stolen from us and is not taken away from us. And everybody knows what I'm talking about."³

Trump's unsubstantiated claims of impending voter fraud in areas with large Democratic constituencies was a constant theme of the campaign. He suggested without evidence that in states without voter ID, many people were impersonating other voters and that "people that have died 10 years ago are still voting." He frequently claimed that the system was "rigged," a term he and his supporters applied to everything from supposedly stolen elections to "skewed" voting machines to the media and the Republican Party establishment conspiring against him. But by the end of the campaign, Trump seemed to focus most of his "rigged" comments on the supposed scourge of voter fraud, which he could explain to his audience with not-so-subtle winks and nods. On October 16, 2016, he tweeted, "The election is absolutely being rigged by the dishonest and distorted media pushing Crooked Hillary—but also at many polling places—SAD."⁴

Even Republican leaders called out Trump's outlandish and unsupported voter fraud claims, provoking this tweeted response: "Of course there is large scale voter fraud happening on and before election day. Why do Republican leaders deny what is going on? So naive!" His surrogate campaigner Rudy Giuliani defended this message, telling CNN's *State of the Union* program: "I'm sorry, dead people generally vote for Democrats rather than Republicans. . . . You want me to [say] that I think the election in Philadelphia and Chicago is going to be fair? I would have to be a moron to say that."⁵

In addition to hyping the supposed dangers of voter fraud from urban areas such as Philadelphia, Trump's campaign created a sign-up sheet on his campaign website for supporters to organize to watch for supposed fraud at the polls. Trump allies such as Roger Stone Jr. also purported to set up "poll watching activities" via the website

Then presidential candidate Donald J. Trump tweet, October 17, 2016

StoptheSteal.org. It was not clear whether these were serious efforts or just means to raise funds, rile up supporters, and collect names, but Trump never sent poll watchers to the polls in 2016.[6]

Trump frequently wrapped his voter fraud claims in innuendo, suggesting he wanted his supporters to take some unspecified action to intimidate minority voters. At an August 2016 rally before a mostly white crowd in Akron, Ohio, he ended his long speech with the statement: "You've got to get every one of your friends. You've got to get every one of your family. You've got to get everybody to go out and watch, and go out and vote. . . . And when I say 'watch,' you know what I'm talking about. Right? You know what I'm talking about. I think you've got to go out and you've got to watch."[7]

Some of Trump's supporters knew what he was talking about. According to a suit later filed by Democrats, "one gentleman from Ohio indicated that he was planning on going to voting precincts to engage in 'racial profiling' to make those voters 'a little bit nervous.' Another man posted on Twitter that he was going to be watching for 'shenanigans' and 'haul [] away' certain voters. The tweet included a picture of a pickup truck with a cage built into the bed."[8]

Perhaps most disconcerting, even beyond the veiled exhortations to violence and intimidation at polling places, Trump relied on his claim of a rigged or stolen election to refuse to promise to abide by the results if he lost to Hillary Clinton. On October 20, 2016, at a rally in Delaware, Ohio, he declared: "Ladies and Gentleman: I want to make a major announcement today. I would like to promise and pledge to all of my voters and supporters, and to all the people of the United States, that I will totally accept the results of this great and historic presidential election—if I win." His dramatic pause before "if I win" was followed by Trump pointing to the crowd and offering a big smile, so that everyone knew that this was his punch line.[9]

The night before, in his final debate with Hillary Clinton, Trump had dodged a question about the election's legitimacy—a question that would never have been asked of any other major presidential candidate in the last century. He refused to promise that he would concede if he lost, saying only: "I will keep you in suspense."[10]

After making the dramatic "if I win" statement at the Ohio rally, Trump returned to the theme of voter fraud: "Of course, I would accept a clear election result, but I would also reserve my right to contest or file a legal challenge in the case of a questionable result. . . . And always, I will follow and abide by all of the rules and traditions of all of the many candidates who have come before me. Always." How much was bravado, and how much was serious? He always spoke in code, maintaining plausible deniability in case things went south, as they sometimes did, violently, at his MAGA rallies.

Trump's focus on "rigged" elections likely polled well with his supporters. Political scientists Kirby Goidel, Keith Gaddie, and Spencer Goidel found that "Republicans and Independents who believed that elections were rigged via voter fraud or media bias were more likely to report that they intended to vote or had already voted. Democrats and Independents who believed that Hillary Clinton would benefit from voter fraud or media bias were more likely to vote for Donald Trump."[11]

After the election, Trump pushed hard on the theme that millions of noncitizens illegally voted for Clinton, offering this wildly improbable scenario as the explanation for his popular vote loss. His tying together of anti-immigrant sentiment and voter fraud was no accident. Research by Adriano Udani and David Kimball found that anti-immigrant attitudes are a strong predictor of voter fraud beliefs and support for voting restrictions. The voter fraud theme fit in well with the nativist sentiment of Trump's presidency.[12]

As we saw in chapter 2, Trump returned to the theme of stolen elections in 2018, claiming that Brenda Snipes in Broward County and other Florida Democrats were trying to steal the U.S. Senate seat from Rick Scott. The sequel to 2016's "horror show" in Philadelphia was the "horrible history" of Brenda Snipes and Broward County in 2018. Both, not coincidentally, involved unsubstantiated claims of fraud by people of color.[13]

While mainstream Republicans often distanced themselves from Trump's baseless voter fraud claims in 2016, by 2018 they were more willing to join in. Florida senator Marco Rubio said during the Broward fiasco that "Democrat lawyers . . . are here to change the results of the election and Broward is where they plan to do it." Speaker of the House Paul Ryan obliquely suggested, without proof, that there was fraud in California, as the long vote-counting process there—given the large number of late and absentee ballots thanks to Democratic Party mobilization efforts—caused several congressional races to shift from Republican to Democratic hands. In a public interview with the *Washington Post*'s Paul Kane, Ryan called the changes in vote totals "bizarre" and said, "We had a lot of wins that night, and three weeks later we lost basically every contested California race. This election system they have, I can't begin to understand what ballot harvesting is." Unlike the North Carolina's ballot harvesting problem in Bladen County, Ryan could point to no criminal activity in California's races.[14]

With a history of incendiary rhetoric from Trump, and a Republican Party no longer pushing back on his claims, it was not hard for Trump's opponents to conjure up images of his refusing to concede a close reelection race in 2020, with a potentially violent result. The liberal magazine *Mother Jones* asked readers in 2019 to imagine that "it's the winter of 2020, and Donald Trump—having lost reelection by a margin closer than expected—is in full attack mode, whipping up stories of runaway voter fraud. Local protest groups coalesce around Facebook posts assailing liberals, murderous 'illegals,' feminists. . . . Pizzagate-style conspiracy theories race through these groups, inflaming their more extreme members. Add a population that is . . . armed to the teeth, and the picture gets pretty dark."[15]

Donald Trump was hardly the first Republican to use claims of voter fraud and stolen elections to intimidate minority voters and shore up the Republican base. In 1981, the Democratic National Committee sued the Republican National Committee in a federal court in New Jersey, claiming intimidation of minority voters in violation of the Voting Rights Act. As the court later recounted, "The RNC sent sample ballots to areas where a large portion of the voters were ethnic minorities, then asked that the name of each voter whose ballot was returned as undeliverable be removed from New Jersey's voter rolls. In addition, in an alleged effort of intimidation, the RNC hired off-duty law enforcement officers to patrol polling places in minority precincts. The officers wore armbands that read: 'National Ballot Security Task Force,' and some carried two-way radios and firearms."[16] Rather than taking the DNC's claims to trial, the RNC settled the case and agreed to a "consent decree," a court order embodying the parties' agreement, which could be enforced through the court's contempt power. The RNC agreed not to engage in certain "ballot security" measures such as "vote-caging" efforts, which target mail at minority communities to ferret out nonresponding voters for removal from the voting rolls. The decree applied only to the national political parties, and not to state and local branches of the Republican Party outside New Jersey. It outlasted Dickinson R. Debevoise, the original federal district court judge on the case, who died in August 2015. John Vasquez, an Obama appointee, then took over and saw the case to its conclusion.

Republican conduct from the 1980s to the 2000s led to frequent clashes between the two parties in federal court over whether the RNC was violating the consent decree. In 1987, Democrats accused the RNC of working with Louisiana Republicans on continued vote caging. "Discovery uncovered the fact that the RNC's Midwest Political Director had remarked that the voter challenge list could 'keep the black vote down considerably.'" In the face of this evidence, the parties' modified consent decree recognized "the importance of neither using, nor appearing to use, racial or ethnic criteria in connection with ballot integrity, ballot security or other efforts to prevent or remedy suspected vote fraud."

Yet in 1990 the DNC was back before the judge, arguing that a North Carolina Republican vote-caging effort targeted African Americans. The court found that this was the work of the state party, not the

RNC, but ruled that the RNC violated the decree by not educating state parties about what constituted unlawful practices under the decree.

There were further clashes in the 2000s, including a 2008 claim alleging that Republicans in New Mexico had hired private investigators to examine voter backgrounds to prepare for challenges to voters' eligibility. The court rejected the Democrats' argument that the conduct violated the decree, finding that the RNC was not involved but that the New Mexico Republican Party, not bound by the consent decree, might have engaged in illegal activity. The consistent theme of these skirmishes was that members of the Republican Party were engaging in conduct that would have violated the decree had it been done by the RNC organization, but the RNC was not responsible for the actions of state and local party organizations.

The RNC began pushing to have the consent decree removed or loosened. The court eventually agreed to loosen it, and it set an expiration date of December 17, 2017, unless the DNC could prove new violations. The RNC failed to convince the U.S. Court of Appeals for the Third Circuit or the Supreme Court to reverse the District Court's decision to leave the modified decree in place through 2017.[17]

With all of Donald Trump's statements and exhortations about voter fraud in the 2016 elections, Democrats were looking for a way to tie Trump's conduct to the RNC so that a court would conclude that the RNC was violating the decree and extend it at least through 2020. The problem was that even though the RNC was of course working with Trump to get him elected president, there was no evidence of coordination on any "ballot security" activities, such as the poll-watching sign-up portion of Trump's campaign web page or Trump's inflammatory rhetoric about "watching" at the polls.

Democrats thought they had caught a break in November 2017, soon before the decree was to expire, when *GQ* magazine quoted Sean

Spicer admitting that on Election Night 2016, he and others "gathered on the fifth floor of Trump Tower in what could be described as basically an oversized utility room." *Politico* recognized that Spicer admitted to a potential violation of the consent decree. Although he later became Trump's press secretary, he was working for the RNC (not Trump) during the campaign, and the fifth floor of Trump Tower was the site of the Trump campaign's poll-monitoring operations. The consent decree prohibited the RNC from contributing to that activity. Spicer supposedly entered the fifth floor despite a sign strictly prohibiting RNC officials from entering the area. Democrats went back to court after Spicer gave the *GQ* interview, claiming a violation.[18]

Over the next year, Democrats and Republicans sparred over whether Spicer's actions were enough to force the RNC to participate in additional discovery to find potential violations of the consent decree. The court allowed limited discovery and the trial court found no smoking gun. It concluded that although the Trump campaign and RNC were working closely together to get Trump and other Republicans elected in 2016, the Trump campaign's claims of voter fraud in minority communities and its voter intimidation were separate from the RNC's actions, and there was no evidence the RNC had violated the decree.

The Third Circuit affirmed the decision, formally ending the consent decree, which had been in place for thirty-five years. But the court, in an opinion it designated as not important enough to justify publication in the official reports, despite its national importance, also pointedly noted the independent "voter suppression tactics endorsed by the Trump campaign." It cited the statements Trump made at his rallies and the "election observer" sign-up spots on his campaign website. The thirty-five-year decree ended with a whimper.[19]

The 2020 election season was the first one in decades to open without the consent decree's protection for minority voters. Meanwhile,

Trump had moved quickly after the 2016 elections to purge the RNC leadership of those who opposed him, replacing them with loyalists. *Politico* reported that he was able to install loyalists in the state parties as well, further consolidating his power over both the national and state Republican organizations.[20]

While *Mother Jones*'s scenario of an armed insurrection by Trump supporters following a 2020 presidential election loss is hopefully no more than a nightmare, it is far more likely that Trump will weaponize the RNC, now freed from the consent decree, to engage in "ballot security" measures aimed at limiting the registration and voting of minorities who are the most reliable Democratic voters. The RNC is also free to coordinate these efforts with state and local political parties.

Trump's half-baked attempts to organize poll watching through his website—which may have been no more than a means to collect the names of people to solicit for donations—could be replaced with a more organized effort via Trumpist-dominated arms of the Republican Party to push the "stolen election" and voter fraud rhetoric toward new efforts at voter suppression. Trumpist Republicans could then seek to delegitimize any Democratic victory in the 2020 elections by claiming that it was procured by voter fraud. These prospects are scary enough, but certainly not at the outer bounds of where Trump's dangerous rhetoric might lead.

I wasn't expecting to be attacked on Twitter by Alec Baldwin.

I had just written an article for *Slate* about the controversial 2018 Georgia gubernatorial race pitting the Republican secretary of state Brian Kemp against Democratic challenger and voting rights activist Stacey Abrams. As we saw in chapter 2, in the weeks before the election Kemp had falsely and recklessly accused Democrats of hacking into the Georgia voter registration database, and posted that accusation on the home page of the official Secretary of State website that voters used to find out where and how to vote. I had called Kemp out about that in an earlier *Slate* piece.[21]

But Kemp had also done much more, from mishandling the state's election security to enacting policies that made it much harder for Georgia voters to register to vote and stay on the rolls. Democrats were understandably apoplectic about Abrams's narrow loss under these circumstances. Election losers increasingly suspect unfair election procedures rather than lower support as an explanation for their losses, and Kemp's actions further undermined confidence in the fairness of the process.[22]

But some of the Democrats' rhetoric was overheated. U.S. senator Sherrod Brown, a Democrat from Ohio, was not alone in calling the Georgia race "stolen." Brown made the remarks in a speech before the Reverend Al Sharpton's National Action Network. And Abrams herself, while recognizing Kemp as the legal winner of the election, repeatedly refused to call the election "legitimate" when pressed by CNN's Jake Tapper. In an April 2019 interview with the *New York Times*, she tried to have it both ways. She defended her earlier statement that she actually "won" her election but also said, "I have no empirical evidence that I would have achieved a higher number of votes."[23]

These statements concerned me, because they went beyond the usual Democratic rhetoric from people like Senators Bernie Sanders and Elizabeth Warren that the "system" was "rigged" against the little guy. Sanders and Warren were usually talking about economic inequality, not the legitimacy of elections. The remarks about the Kemp-Abrams race were different.[24]

So I wrote another piece for *Slate,* "Why Democrats Should Not Call the Georgia Governor's Race 'Stolen,'" and the reaction was unlike anything I had ever seen from the left. I am used to being attacked by folks on the right, but not by people like the actor Alec Baldwin, who often played a vicious and stupid Donald Trump character on *Saturday Night Live*, or the actor and activist Patricia Arquette.[25]

Baldwin tweeted a link to my piece, with the following message going to his 1.1 million followers: "Wherein @rickhasen lays out his 'guns don't kill people' pablum re 'voter suppression doesn't effect elections. The lack of votes for your candidate does.' This . . . is . . . ridiculous. And, no, don't stop saying Kemp is illegitimate."[26]

Once *New York Times* reporter Maggie Haberman sent out a link to the piece via Twitter, things really exploded. Actor Patricia Arquette replied, "It was stolen. Enough with worrying about looking like sore losers." After I noted that some people on Twitter were calling me a Nazi or a member of the KKK, others responded, "You're not a Nazi. Pro-voter suppression apologist is closer" and "I don't think you're a Nazi. I think you are a fool and a coward."[27]

I hope that many who attacked me saw no more than the headline in a tweet or news summary and did not reject the substance of my argument, which raised three points about why stolen election rhetoric is dangerous and unjustified. None of it involved worry about looking like a sore loser.[28]

First, rhetoric about stolen elections feeds a growing cycle of mistrust and delegitimization of the election process, an attack pushed by President Trump and other Republicans who have begun yelling "voter fraud" when they are behind in the count. There is reason to fear that Trump could refuse to concede the 2020 presidential election—or even declare himself the winner—if he is ahead or even close behind on Election Night and the results inevitably shift toward Democrats as the counting continues. After all, Trump declared himself "exoner-

> **HABFoundation** ✓
> @ABFalecbaldwin
>
> Follow ⌄
>
> Wherein @rickhasen lays out his "guns don't kill people" pablum re "voter suppression doesn't effect elections. The lack of votes for your candidate does."
>
> This...is...ridiculous.
>
> And, no, don't stop saying Kemp is illegitimate.
>
> **Why Democrats Should Not Call the Georgia Governor's Ra...**
> There are three important reasons to cool this rhetoric, despite Brian Kemp's odious voter suppression efforts.
> apple.news
>
> 4:27 PM - 18 Nov 2018
>
> **12** Retweets **57** Likes
>
> 💬 10   🔁 12   ♡ 57   ✉

Alec Baldwin tweet, November 18, 2018

ated" after Attorney General William Barr issued his summary of Mueller's report, which said that Trump was *not* exonerated.[29]

A democratic polity depends on losers accepting election results, even if the election was not conducted perfectly. It is important to reserve "stolen" election rhetoric for conduct even more outrageous than Kemp's. His decisions, while odious, either have not been ruled illegal or were allowed by courts to remain in place for the 2018 election. The election fraud in North Carolina's Ninth Congressional District election in 2018 is the most prominent recent example of an election tainted enough by malfeasance that it could have justifiably been called "stolen" had the beneficiary of the chicanery, Mark Harris, been seated.

Second, the charge of a stolen election is unproven. Although Hillary Clinton declared in November 2018 that if Abrams "had a fair election she already would have won," and California senator Kamala Harris tweeted in May 2019, "Let's say this loud and clear—without voter suppression: @staceyabrams is Governor Stacey Abrams," we do not know that Kemp's suppression efforts cost Abrams the seat. As Ari Berman put it, "We don't know yet—and might never know—how many people were disenfranchised or dissuaded from voting in the state. But it's clear that Kemp did everything in his power to put in place restrictive voting policies that would help his candidacy and hurt his opponent, all while overseeing his own election."[30]

And so it was profoundly disappointing to see Stacey Abrams declare without sufficient evidence in a March 2019 speech that "I did win my election, I just didn't get to have the job." She pulled back a bit in a speech in April, declaring: "And so in response to what I believe was a stolen election, and I'm not saying they stole it from me. They stole it from the voters of Georgia. I cannot prove empirically that I would've won, but we will never know."[31]

Saying Kemp suppressed or tried to suppress Democratic votes and saying the election was "stolen" are two different things, and when Democrats raise charges of a stolen election that cannot be proved, they undermine their complaints about suppressive tactics. If Democrats cannot prove suppression determined the outcome, some people will mistakenly think the suppression is no big deal.

The final problem with "stolen election" rhetoric is that it focuses attention on the wrong question: whether there was enough suppression to change election outcomes. The right question is why the state gets to put stumbling blocks in front of voters—such as onerous voter registration requirements and easy voter purge rules—without offering good reasons for doing so. We know that the "voter fraud" and public confidence arguments often advanced to support suppressive tactics are bogus, and we need to keep saying it, whether it is one voter facing new hurdles or thousands.

By focusing on the dignity and respect afforded to each voter, we can push to maximize the number of eligible voters who are able to cast a ballot that will count, regardless of election outcomes. Maybe this argument makes me a fool and a coward; I still doubt it makes me a Nazi.

Although Abrams tried to thread a very thin needle in saying that Brian Kemp's election was legal but not necessarily "legitimate," what she did after the election was much more productive. She and her legal allies in the voting rights community filed a massive lawsuit alleging that various components of Georgia's election process acted synergistically to violate the constitutional and voting rights of Georgia voters. The lawsuit attacks Georgia's strict voter purges, which the complaint says were timed with Kemp's own elections; its "exact match" policy, which has kept thousands of voters off the registration rolls for discrepancies on voting forms and driving records as minor as a missing hyphen; its insecure voter registration database software and voting machinery, which are vulnerable to hacking and lack backup paper records; its closing and moving of polling places; its inaccurate voter registration rolls; its inadequate oversight over the casting of provisional ballots; and its management of the dissemination, processing, and counting of absentee ballots—including the state's failure to notify voters of problems with their ballots that could have been cured in time for the vote to be counted.[32]

Rather than focusing on just one of the hurdles facing voters, this suit laid out all of them together. Voting should not be an obstacle course, but the lawsuit claims that's exactly what Georgia created through a combination of incompetence and intentional suppression.

It remains unclear whether such a lawsuit will succeed in taking down the worst elements of Georgia's voting system. But it is a productive way to channel anger over suppressive tactics, and, unlike "stolen" election rhetoric, it seems unlikely to erode voter confidence in election results. Research shows that the higher the level of competence in election administration, the more confidence voters will have in the fairness of the results. Successful lawsuits to challenge bad election administration help to improve voter confidence and counteract some of the overheated rhetoric.[33]

So let's flip the script on the "Trump won't concede if he loses" fears and imagine that Trump narrowly wins reelection in 2020 thanks to victories in Georgia, Florida, and Texas, each of which has restrictive voting laws. Should we be just as worried about the fragility of our republic if many Democrats believe that the 2020 election, like the 2018 election in Georgia, was stolen, even if there is no proof that these laws were responsible for the results? What will this mean when the claims of illegitimacy are fanned by outside actors via social media to organize street protests? What reaction would that provoke from Trump, who has emergency powers and can declare martial law? As with the *Mother Jones* Trump scenario, the picture gets dark pretty quickly.

It bears repeating that our democracy depends on confidence in the fairness of the vote, and on the losers' acceptance of election results. Until very recently, this point was so obvious that it was hardly discussed in relation to the United States, but the time for that discussion has come. Electoral losers in the hyperpolarized United States already have less confidence in the fairness of the electoral process than electoral winners. Incendiary rhetoric only adds to the suspicion. We play with fire when we use language that tends to undermine the voter confidence that remains.[34]

5

Surviving 2020 and Beyond

"We have to inoculate against that, we have to be prepared for that."[1]

In May 2019, Nancy Pelosi gave an extraordinary interview to *New York Times* reporter Glenn Thrush in which she expressed concern that President Trump might not leave office voluntarily if defeated in 2020. Pelosi, a Democratic representative in Congress since 1987 and the first woman to serve as Speaker of the House, told Thrush that Democrats should run a center-left campaign in 2020 and not try to impeach Trump, despite the findings in the Mueller report, so that they could win a wide victory over the incumbent president. But it was what she said about the peaceful transition of power that caught the nation's attention.

The only way to ensure Trump's removal from office in 2020, Pelosi said, was if the Democratic presidential candidate won an overwhelming victory. She revealed that she had told her inner circle before the 2018 midterm elections that she was worried Trump would try to stop a Democratic takeover of the House of Representatives if that election was close: "If we win by four seats, by a thousand votes each, he's not going to respect the election. . . . He would poison the public mind. He would challenge each of the races; he would say you can't seat these people. . . . We had to win. Imagine if we hadn't won—oh, don't even imagine. So, as we go forward, we have to have the same approach."

That Pelosi would publicly make such statements was a remarkable acknowledgment of the new dangers facing the United States. And she was not alone in her concerns. Michael Cohen, President Trump's former lawyer and fixer, concluded a long day of public testimony in February 2019 before the House Oversight Committee by remarking, "Given my experience working for Mr. Trump, I fear that if he loses the election in 2020 that there will never be a peaceful transition of power, and this is why I agreed to appear before you today."[2]

The testimony by Cohen, now a Trump opponent who was just weeks away from beginning a three-year prison term for financial crimes and campaign finance violations, mostly involved Trump's business and political practices. The hearing did not really deal with his extensive but legal norm-breaking and embrace of authoritarian tactics, such as calling the free press the "true enemy of the people," and so Cohen's statement about Trump's potentially refusing to give up power seemed to come out of nowhere.[3]

Cohen's years of experience by Trump's side may have given him unique insight into the man's psyche, but the concern that Trump would try to cling to power if he lost the 2020 election—or if he appeared to lose but nonetheless claimed victory—has been widespread among his opponents. It is a belief fueled by comments like those we saw in the last chapter, such as his toying suggestion that he would not accept his opponent's victory in 2016, as well as by his general rejection of the norms by which people in power speak of the democratic process. The *Mother Jones* scenario of a potential armed insurrection should Trump refuse to concede did not seem implausible to many of his opponents.

The concern was not helped by a somewhat questionable 2017 poll showing that a majority of Republicans would support postponing the 2020 elections if Trump said it was necessary to make sure only eligible voters participated. Nor was it helped by a 2019 statement from the Trump reelection campaign's national press secretary, Kayleigh McEnany, attacking House Democrats' investigations into Trump's financial dealings, connections to Russia, and other matters as an "abuse of power." The statement concluded: "These desperate Democrats know they cannot beat President Trump in 2020, so instead they have embarked on a disgraceful witch hunt with one singular aim: topple the will of the American people and seize the power that they have zero chance at winning legitimately." The message echoed an earlier tweet from President Trump: "The Dems are trying to win an election in 2020 that they know they cannot legitimately win!" Then there was Trump's frequent joking that he might stay in office for more than two terms.[4]

The anxiety about Trump in 2016 was serious enough that the Obama administration came up with contingency plans. *New York* magazine reported that the plan "called for congressional Republicans, former presidents, and former Cabinet-level officials including Colin Powell and Condoleezza Rice, to try and forestall a political crisis by validating the election result. In the event that Trump tried to dispute a Clinton victory, they would affirm the result as well as the conclusions reached by the U.S. intelligence community that Russian interference in the election sought to favor Trump, and not Clinton."[5]

The 2018 publication of *How Democracies Die* by political scientists Steven Levitsky and Daniel Ziblatt accelerated worries about Trump's lack of commitment to the democratic process. The authors, comparing democratic countries that had slid into authoritarianism with those that avoided doing so, warned of the need for political parties to isolate and reject authoritarians, whom they classified as possessing "four behavioral warning signs. . . . We should worry when a politician 1) rejects, in words or action, the democratic rules of the game, 2) denies the legitimacy of opponents, 3) tolerates or encourages violence, or 4) indicates a willingness to curtail civil liberties of opponents, including the media." Trump, the authors showed, exhibited all of these attributes, and the Republican Party, far from pushing back, had acquiesced in a hostile takeover. They pointed to the establishment of the Pence-Kobach voter fraud commission as one of the most important signs of Trump's authoritarian tendencies.[6]

And yet Trump often spoke in code, and despite verbally attacking democratic institutions that could hold him accountable, such as the free press, the courts, Congress, and the FBI, he mostly did not follow through with action. He let the Pence-Kobach commission collapse. This inability or unwillingness to act on his impulses convinced some that Trump was a fundamentally weak president, a big talker who would not actually upset a peaceful transition to power in the event he narrowly lost. Many Trump supporters and some "Never Trump" conservatives believed that his opponents overstated the dangers of his norm breaking and lack of commitment to democratic values. Instead, they said, the opponents themselves had broken norms by relentlessly attacking Trump and seeking to undermine his presidency.[7]

Whether or not Trump poses an actual authoritarian danger to the peaceful transition of power, Trumpism and the Trump presidency have awakened public understanding that peaceful transitions via elections cannot be taken for granted. We must work continuously to shore up democratic institutions, technology, procedures, and rules. This lesson extends beyond the 2020 elections through our current period of hyperpolarization, rapid technological change, economic upheaval, and shifting domestic and geopolitical alliances.

The Trump-declaring-victory-while-losing scenario is not the only way to imagine an election meltdown in 2020 or in a future presidential election. Another plausible scenario, outlined in chapter 3, is an Election Day attack on the power grid in a swing state Democratic city like Detroit. Or imagine massively long lines in African American parts of Georgia thanks to breakdowns of new voting machines, or election administration snafus that Democratic voters worry have skewed the state's Electoral College vote toward Republicans. What if rapidly spreading vituperative social media posts claiming that Republican malfeasance has cost Democrats the election inflame Democrats to refuse to accept a narrow Republican victory? As Norm Ornstein has put it, without a "Plan B" to deal with such disruptions, things can easily move from election snafu to constitutional crisis.[8]

Below I lay out a number of practical medium-term and longer-term measures to deal with the perpetual threat of election meltdown in the United States. All of them should be implemented to minimize the serious risks faced by our democracy. Some of the medium-term solutions could be implemented by 2020, although political stalemate makes that unlikely.

Unfortunately, coming up with short-term solutions to defuse potential nightmare 2020 scenarios in a Trumpian polarized society is somewhat of a fool's errand. My proposals for longer-term changes, such as improved civics education, feel a little like putting a band-aid on a gunshot wound.

Consider three possible short-term fixes for a 2020 stalemate, and the problems with each:

- *Following the Obama plan, responsible bipartisan leaders trot out elders such as former secretaries of state Colin Powell and Madeleine Albright to call for calm and the acceptance of election results.* It is very hard to imagine that anything said by these former leaders would sway ardent Trump supporters, or Democrats who believe that the party has lain down too often in the face of Republican hardball tactics. Our politics has hardened since Al Gore quickly gave up his 2000 election contest after the Supreme Court ruled for Bush in *Bush v. Gore,* and the country mostly moved on. Social media–fueled anger and resentment could easily lead to a deeper and scarier partisan divide over an election dispute.

- *The country defers to the courts, including the Supreme Court, to decide a disputed election result fairly and in accordance with the rule of law.* One may wonder, given the increasing partisan divide on the Supreme Court, whether the Court could move beyond politics and decide issues fairly, neutrally, and ideally (for the sake of legitimacy) unanimously. Neutrality might be too much to ask, given the Court's performance in *Bush v. Gore* and its increasing political polarization since then. And I do not expect Democrats to accept the Supreme Court's ruling if the Republican-appointed Court majority resolves the election in favor of the Republican candidate over the four Democratic-appointed justices' objections. Democrats are already calling for "packing the courts" by adding more (Democratic-appointed) justices. They are unlikely to defer to Neil Gorsuch, whom they see as having taken a "stolen" seat from President Obama's nominee Merrick Garland, who never received a hearing.[9]

Even putting aside the increasing partisanship that has infected the judiciary, the view that courts can solve most problems by applying neutral legal principles falls apart when there is no clear law to apply. Absent a "Plan B" under state law for rerunning a disrupted election or resolving complicated ballot disputes in time for the counting of Electoral College votes, courts may be working without a net—and without clear guidance on the rules, the judges' ideological predispositions can easily fill the vacuum created by laws' absence. In order for courts to be able to do their jobs effectively *after* the election, states will have needed to act *before* the election to shore up their laws and adopt principles for resolving election disputes, such as the American Law Institute's suggested principles for resolving disputed presidential elections.[10]

• *Massive street protests are organized to get a fair counting and resolution of the dispute.* In theory, public protests could move decision makers to resolve a disputed election fairly if there is an outcry over how an election was won, or to force a concession by a candidate who has refused to concede despite strong evidence of a winner. But in a hyperpolarized environment, such protests raise the risk of political violence—the *Mother Jones* nightmare of armed protesters and militias that President Trump has sometimes encouraged with his rhetoric. Any attempt to organize those with legitimate grievances about how officials are purporting to resolve a disputed election is likely to face counter-protests organized through social media. There is no reason to think that only one side would take to the streets.

The bottom line is that there are no miracle cures. I can see no easy way out should the election be extremely close or targeted for manipulation of the results. That is why it is all the more important to focus *now* on the steps that can be taken to lessen the risks of meltdown.

Medium-term solutions should combat the four great threats to the fairness and stability of the American electoral process—voter suppression, pockets of election administrator incompetence, dirty tricks, and incendiary rhetoric. Separately and synergistically, these threats undermine voters' trust that election results reflect the will of the people.

Combating Voter Suppression

The media often frame the voting wars as a stalemate between claims of voter fraud and voter suppression, but it is time to declare the battle over. The issue of organized voter fraud has now been put to the test in courts and in social science, and there is no proof that it is any kind of serious problem in the United States. Just as important, the few categories of fraud that occasionally affect election outcomes, such as absentee ballot fraud, have not been the target of voter suppression efforts like voter ID laws and overly aggressive voter roll purges.

On the other side of the ledger, there is no longer a question that some laws making it harder to register and vote serve no legitimate purpose and are motivated by an attempt to suppress (usually Democratic) turnout. Some of these laws seem to have little or no effect, despite occasional hyperbolic statements to the contrary, and their opponents should be careful to avoid making excessive claims in the absence of good evidence. Other laws, such as Kansas's law requiring documentary proof of citizenship, can disenfranchise tens of thousands of voters. Either way, states should have no ability to make it harder for eligible voters to register and vote without coming forward with very strong reasons.

Scholars, lawyers, and those in the public sphere must continue to speak out against voter suppression laws, even at the risk of being labeled "raw enemy activists" who would permit voter fraud to run rampant. The voter fraud shibboleth should no longer be accepted in polite conversation as just one side of a two-sided debate. It is a sham perpetrated by people who should know better, advanced for political advantage.

Courts remain open to claims against harsh voting rules, and it appears, at least for now, that they will reject some but not all of the most blatant suppression attempts that serve no legitimate purpose. The courts blocked Kansas's law, but they allowed North Dakota to put in place a "residence address" requirement for voter identification that seemed plainly calculated to make it harder for Native Americans to vote. As the Supreme Court becomes dominated by conservative justices, especially justices who seem willing to countenance President Trump's partisan impulses on issues like the Muslim travel ban or the citizenship question on the 2020 census form, efforts to stop many of these laws under the Voting Rights Act and other federal statutes face increasingly uphill climbs.

With judicial recourse likely to be partially effective at best, many of these battles will have to be fought in state legislatures and, in states that allow it, through voter initiatives. Democrats have learned that campaigning on voter suppression works, for the simple reason that people are offended by efforts to make it harder for them or their friends, relatives, and allies to vote. Voting rights has become a political issue like health care or climate change. The shift toward Democrats in states such as North Carolina was partially a reaction to Republican legislative overreach on voting rules and procedures. The issue of voting rights has caused people to take to the streets, as North Carolina residents did in their "Moral Mondays" marches.[11]

Lawsuits and political organizing must go hand in hand in combating rules aimed at trying to make it harder to register and to vote. Unless and until the Republican Party again becomes willing to compete for the votes of minority voters rather than suppress them, Republican-led state and local governments will be continually tempted to pass laws making voting and registration harder.

Fixing Election Administrator Incompetence

As much as Democrats and those on the left are happy to call out Republican voter suppression, they need to do much more to eliminate pockets of election administrator incompetence in large Democratic cities and elsewhere. Most election administrators do a very good job, especially given their resource constraints, and a 2018 survey by the Pew Research Center found that "nearly nine-in-ten (89%) have confidence in poll workers in their community to do a good job, and majorities say the same about local and state election officials." The sky is not falling when it comes to how elections are run in most places, and hyperbole to the contrary is unhelpful.[12]

Instead, reform efforts should focus on pockets of incompetence. It should not have taken a Republican governor to remove Brenda Snipes as head of Broward County's elections. She should have lost to a Democratic opponent in an election. Democrats should cooperate with Republicans to remove election administrators who repeatedly make major errors or who allow their election systems to fall into disrepair, as in Detroit. Sometimes a place simply needs more resources, but significant problems across repeated elections in the same jurisdiction are often a sign of incompetence. Another such sign is bureaucratic resistance to efforts to assure transparency in how voting is conducted.

Adequate voter list maintenance makes sense for a working voter registration process, even if it is pushed hard by the fraudulent fraud squad for the wrong reasons. The more that can be done to eliminate problems before the election, the less room there will be after a close election to question procedures and discretionary choices.

Everyone should support efforts such as the Presidential Commission on Election Administration and the work of the Bipartisan Policy Center to push for better technology such as the use of online voter registration, dissemination of best practices, and continued professionalization of election administration. The Electronic Registration Information Center, or ERIC, now includes twenty-two states and Washington, D.C., cooperating to keep voter registration information updated across states. It is hard to think of something less sexy than focusing on electoral competence rather than voter suppression, but in the end, many more votes may be saved by competent election administration than by stopping voter ID laws.[13]

The Elections Clause in Article I of the Constitution gives Congress the power to impose minimal competency standards on states for the conduct of congressional elections, and Congress should act to do so. The last time Congress took a big step in that direction was after the 2000 presidential election debacle in Florida, when it passed the Help America Vote Act of 2002. Among other things, HAVA provided a large pot of money for voting machine upgrades and set standards for the machines' reliability. As a result, we lose many fewer votes to bad machinery than we used to.

HAVA also created the U.S. Election Assistance Commission to certify the reliability of voting machines and serve as a clearinghouse for best practices. Unfortunately, the agency has been hobbled from the start by resistance from state election officials and House Republicans. For years it lacked a quorum of commissioners, and it only regained that quorum in 2019 after House Speaker Paul Ryan inexplicably blocked the renomination of Commissioner Matthew Masterson, a Republican appointee widely respected by Democrats and Republicans as an expert on election cybersecurity, and the president came forward with new nominees. Masterson continues to work on these issues at the Department of Homeland Security, and others have been appointed to fill the open spots at the commission. Whether the commission can play a constructive role going forward is uncertain, especially given questions about one of the new Republican commissioners, Donald Palmer, and his role in helping to foster hysteria about noncitizen voting.[14]

Congress could do much more to empower the commission to help with election administration and cybersecurity. One of the biggest issues now is whether the new generation of voting machines coming on line, ballot marking devices, or BMDs, which print a voter's ballot complete with a bar code that is read by ballot-counting machines, can be fairly audited to assure that vote totals are accurate and there has been no hacking of the machinery. A strong Commission could impose federal standards for BMDs.[15]

Combating Dirty Tricks

Much of the work to protect the American electoral system from hacking requires years of effort before and between elections. It begins by recognizing, as the Department of Homeland Security did in the waning days of the Obama administration, that the electoral process is "critical infrastructure" that needs continual attention from national security professionals. Despite the long American tradition of state and local control, even over federal elections, Article I gives Congress ample power to require that states cooperate in protecting voter registration databases, voting technology, and infrastructure.

There is a bit of room for optimism here. Even U.S. Election Assistance Commission chairwoman Christy McCormick, who in 2017 called claims of Russian interference in the 2016 elections "deceptive propaganda perpetrated on the American public" by the Obama administration and who appeared to have been put on the Election Assistance Commission by Senate Republicans to stymie its work improving election processes, came around in 2019 to support cooperation between states and the federal government on election cybersecurity. It was quite a change for the only federal election official to serve on the disingenuous Pence-Kobach voter fraud commission. After having been asked numerous times by reporter Jessica Huseman if she "had rethought her initial denial that Russia intervened in the 2016 election," McCormick ultimately could not ignore the overwhelming evidence of interference.[16]

Perhaps after Trump is out of office and the Russia investigation has faded from view, Democrats and Republicans can come together to pass stronger legislation, and a new president can push the national security apparatus to protect this critical infrastructure. In the meantime, activists like those in Georgia must be supported when they sue to ensure that states make their voting systems secure and reliable.[17]

Campaigning has been transformed by social media, and efforts to manipulate voter opinion, both through truthful but inflammatory postings and through misinformation, will only increase. Consistent with the First Amendment, Congress can expand disclosure rules to require that those who expend considerable resources on social media efforts aimed to influence American elections reveal their identities and their spending. Congress should also tighten up existing rules that ban some forms of foreign contributions and spending in American elections.[18]

Misinformation remains one of the greatest threats in the social media age, and there is very little the government can do consistent with the First Amendment to stop its spread. Instead, the public should pressure social media corporations like Facebook, Twitter, and Google to put in place strong mechanisms to limit foreign interference in U.S. elections and to flag foreign and domestic sources of misinformation, particularly false information that is amplified via bots and other means. Offering fact checks from reputable sources also may be a means of helping to stop the spread of some misinformation, but a recent report concluded that this is no silver bullet. The problem of false information in campaigns and elections spread via social media is complex and not yet fully understood.[19]

In addition to taking concrete steps to combat political misinformation, Facebook, Google, and now Apple (thanks to its rising Apple News app) need to rethink the social harm of business models that have helped decimate advertising revenue for news media entities. Social media corporations suck much of the revenue from the news business, rendering the traditional business models for news organizations untenable. Alternative financial arrangements are in the public interest to assure that readers and viewers can continue to get reliable information from trusted sources.[20]

For low-tech election crimes, such as the absentee ballot fraud that cropped up in Bladen County, North Carolina, deterrence begins with smart and targeted law enforcement efforts. Investigators in North Carolina saw troubling patterns, but prosecutions took years and began only after the state's Board of Elections refused to certify the results in the 2018 election for the state's Ninth Congressional District.

States should also tighten rules related to the handling of absentee ballots. Consider the question of "ballot harvesting." In some states, such as California, it is now legal for campaigns to send out people to collect the ballots of strangers. On the one hand, allowing campaigns to collect ballots helps elderly and disabled voters as well as those in remote rural areas. On the other hand, this practice allows Bladen-type abuse where unscrupulous people collect blank absentee ballots or steal them from mailboxes and fill them in. We have not seen reports of these types of problems yet in California, but they could arise in the future. For this reason, ballot harvesting should be limited to collection of ballots from those who face difficulties turning in ballots themselves. A signed declaration by the voter stating the need for assistance should be enough to allow for the collection of such ballots.

Combating Incendiary Rhetoric about Stolen Elections

Combating damaging rhetoric about "stolen" or "rigged" elections requires being able to share truthful and reliable information about how elections are conducted and votes are counted. It begins with clear procedures and transparency from elected officials about what is happening in each stage of the process and why. It then must be followed by truthful information from these officials and the news media combating claims of stolen elections with facts.

For example, despite efforts by California election officials to explain before the 2018 elections that it would take weeks to count outstanding absentee and other ballots, we have seen that House Speaker Paul Ryan called the long count "really bizarre" when Republican congressional candidates saw their leads evaporate as this counting proceeded. There was nothing bizarre: late-arriving ballots tend to break for Democrats because of different voting patterns among Democrats and Republicans, and Democrats used an unprecedented ballot harvesting effort to collect absentee ballots. They took advantage of the new law allowing the practice in California, and it led to consistent, unjustified claims of voter fraud and stolen elections from Republicans on the losing side.[21]

Further, even though their efforts may not be fully effective in the heat of a disputed election, bipartisan groups of leaders should organize in advance before each election to be ready to speak up for the rule of law and the peaceful transition of power. Unsupported claims of stolen or rigged elections should be rejected by leaders on both sides of the aisle, and members of Congress should publicly state a commitment to follow the rule of law in the transition period between elections.

Finally, the most important way to shut down the potency of stolen election rhetoric is to take away the bases for suspicion: states should not make it harder to vote for no good reason; incompetent election administrators should be removed from office, and sound election administration principles should be followed nationwide; federal and state governments should continually improve cybersecurity for voting systems and infrastructure; and states should deter and prosecute actual election crimes.

The rest of the work needed to assure peaceful transitions of power via elections in the United States is societal and long term, focusing both on the means by which we conduct our elections and on bolstering voters' democratic competence and respect for the rule of law.

For two decades, I have called for the United States to make fundamental changes in the way we conduct our elections to bring our procedures more in line with international standards. In my 2012 book *The Voting Wars*, I called for "nonpartisan, professionalized election administration at the federal, state, and local levels, with more power in the hands of the federal government than state government and more power in the hands of the states than localities. Neutral election officials, whose allegiance is not to a political party or candidate but to a fair election system, must be the norm." The country has taken no steps in this direction, and no such changes are on the horizon despite continued disputes over partisans running our elections.[22]

I also suggested uniform standards for dealing with absentee and provisional ballots, regular updating of election laws and voting technology, and uniformity and clarity in election rules and policies. On the specific issue of voter registration, I called for federalized, automatic voter registration, for the government to pay all costs associated with identifying voters, and for a unique voter identification number to be assigned to each voter for life. "The government should provide a voter identification card to each voter," I wrote then, "but voters lacking identification would have the choice of using a thumbprint or other means to verify their identity."[23]

We have not moved any closer to this model of standardization and uniformity. Instead, we have seen the emergence of red state election law and blue state election law. Some Republican states have made it harder for people to register and vote, a trend that continues in the run-up to the 2020 elections. Many Democratic states (and some Republican ones) have made voting easier, such as by adopting "automatic" voter registration: requiring state agencies to automatically register eligible persons willing to vote who interact with a government agency such as a department of motor vehicles. We are still a long way away from a system in which eligible adult citizens don't have to worry about voter registration from the moment they become eligible to vote.[24]

Voter competence begins with accurate information, and yet our hyperpolarized social media ecosystem encourages people to live in ideological cocoons increasingly flooded with misinformation. We would not want laws allowing the government to censor posts on social media, even if the First Amendment allowed it. That would surely be a cure worse than the disease. But the dangers of misinformation, rapidly changing technology, and the decline in trust in real news that accompanies the growth of misinformation mean that voters increasingly will struggle to assess the veracity of information.[25]

The longest-term project is civics education for children and adults on the importance of the rule of law, democratic legitimacy, and peaceful transitions to power following fair elections. Political and civic leaders, teachers, and others in the public sphere must foster discussions across platforms and venues about these subjects. This includes discussions about the specific danger of loose talk about "stolen" or "rigged" elections without any proof or even basis in reality.

Civics education faces high hurdles in our media-siloed society, where universities are viewed as taking the liberal side in the culture wars, rendering fact-based arguments a hard sell to the right, and where the left has grown increasingly intolerant of any ideas challenging certain forms of orthodoxy. It is not bothsidesism to recognize that some Republicans have tried to suppress Democratic votes but that there are ways for Democrats to talk about the issue without language that risks delegitimizing the entire political system.

As for assuring peaceful transitions of power, we can think of civics education and the quest for civil, reasoned discourse as a battle of truth against the Donald Trumps of the world, a world in which some of the worst actors have the largest megaphones. Amid the cacophony, we can hope that fair-minded people across the political spectrum understand the dangers to American democracy enough to come together to support institutions like a free press and independent judiciary, and to promote the values of fair debate, due process, checks and balances, and belief in objective truth.

In the end, this form of civics education aims to convince the American public that what unites us and helps us thrive is our multifaceted plural democracy, in which losers respect fair election outcomes and vow to fight another day, and that our democracy's value is much greater than the issues dividing us.

Notes

Introduction

1. "Remarks by President Trump Before Meeting with Vice Premier Liu He of the People's Republic of China," The White House, updated on Feb. 22, 2019, https://www.whitehouse.gov/briefings-statements/remarks-president-trump-meeting-vice-premier-liu-peoples-republic-china-2/ [https://perma.cc/S7BK-VWFW] ("White House").

2. Brian Murphy, *Harris Took a "Step of Faith." Now His Election Must Be Redone, and the Future Is Uncertain,* News & Observer, Feb. 23, 2019, https://www.newsobserver.com/news/politics-government/article226628829.html.

3. Amy Gardner, *N.C. Board Declares a New Election in Contested House Race After GOP Candidate Admitted He Was Mistaken in His Testimony,* Wash. Post, Feb. 21, 2019, https://www.washingtonpost.com/politics/candidate-says-new-congressional-election-warranted-in-north-carolina/2019/02/21/acae4482-35e0-11e9-854a-7a14d7f-ec96a_story.html.

4. The specifics of these allegations are discussed and cited in later book chapters.

5. White House, *supra* note 1. The official White House transcript lists Jackson's interruption as "There haven't been any cases (inaudible)—." The fuller and more accurate statement from Jackson appears in a now-deleted tweet from Hunter Walker, a White House reporter for *Yahoo! News* who was also present at the discussion. A screenshot of @Hunterw, Twitter, Feb. 22, 2019, 4:06 p.m. PST, https://twitter.com/hunterw/status/1099098116303847424?s=21, is posted at https://perma.cc/MC5T-N3R6. Walker also emailed me his notes and confirmed in the email that Hallie Jackson was the reporter. Email from Hunter Walker to author, Apr. 8, 2019 (on file with the author).

6. John Kruzel, *False Facebook Post Claims Million of Fraudulent Votes Cast in California*, PolitiFact, Nov. 6, 2018, https://www.politifact.com/truth-o-meter/statements/2018/nov/06/blog-posting/false-facebook-post-claims-millions-fraudulent-vot/ [https://perma.cc/SD39-ACUG].

7. Associated Press, *California, Legal Group Reach Agreement on Old Voter Records*, Jan. 3, 2019, https://www.apnews.com/66ee694e83d047d5bad19ed4d8ba0418 [https://perma.cc/W32Y-R3M5].

8. @KenPaxtonTX, Twitter, Jan. 25, 2019, 12:37 p.m. PST, https://twitter.com/KenPaxtonTX/status/1088898595653386240 [https://perma.cc/J3JG-SZLF]; Lauren McGaughy, *Texas Attorney General Ken Paxton Won't Go on Trial for Alleged Crimes Before Election Day, Experts Say*, Dallas Morning News, June 29, 2018, https://www.dallasnews.com/news/texas-politics/2018/06/29/texas-attorney-general-ken-paxton-wont-go-trial-alleged-crimes-before-election-day-experts-say; Patrick Svitek & Emma Platoff, *Texas Court of Criminal Appeals Rules against Prosecutors in Ken Paxton Payment Case*, Texas Tribune, Nov. 21, 2018, https://www.texastribune.org/2018/11/21/ken-paxton-texas-criminal-case-attorneys-fees/.

9. Philip Bump, *Trump Lays Some of the Ol' "Both Sides" on Alleged Election Fraud in North Carolina*, Wash. Post, Feb. 22, 2019, https://www.washingtonpost.com/politics/2019/02/22/trump-lays-some-ol-both-sides-alleged-election-fraud-north-carolina/; Philip Bump, *Time and Time Again, Hyped Claims of Rampant Illegal Voting Turn Out to Be Untrue*, Wash. Post, Feb. 5, 2019, https://wapo.st/2Hl9l24. Alexa Ura, *"Someone Did Not Do Their Due Diligence": How an Attempt to Review Texas' Voter Rolls Turned into a Debacle*, Texas Tribune, Feb. 1, 2019, https://www.texastribune.org/2019/02/01/texas-citizenship-voter-roll-review-how-it-turned-boondoggle/; James Barragán, *Failed Secretary of State Nominee David Whitley Back on Gov. Greg Abbott's Payroll*, Dallas Morning News, May 31, 2019, https://www.dallasnews.com/news/politics/2019/05/31/failed-secretary-state-nominee-david-whitley-back-gov-greg-abbotts-payroll; Alexa Ura, *Eight Texas Counties Agree to Halt Voter Citizenship Reviews While Lawsuits Proceed*, Texas Tribune, Feb. 21, 2019, https://www.texastribune.org/2019/02/21/eight-texas-counties-agree-halt-voter-citizenship-reviews-amid-lawsuit/; Carlos Sanchez, *David Whitley's Secretary of State Confirmation May Now Be Doomed*, Texas Monthly, Feb. 22, 2019, https://www.texasmonthly.com/politics/david-whitley-secretary-of-state-nomination-doomed/; Liam Stack, *Texas Ends Review That Questioned Citizenship of Almost 100,000 Voters*, N.Y. Times, Apr. 26, 2019, https://www.nytimes.com/2019/04/26/us/texas-voting.html.

10. Texas LULAC v. Whitley, No. 5:19-cv-00074-FB (W.D. Tex. Feb. 27, 2019), at 1–4. Available at: https://big.assets.huffingtonpost.com/athena/files/2019/02/27/5c76 df91e4b0952f89ddcd34.pdf [https://perma.cc/43GJ-LGLK].

11. Shelby County v. Holder, 570 U.S. 529 (2013).

12. Brianna Sacks & Otillia Steadman, *Inside the North Carolina Republican Vote Machine: Cash, Pills—And Ballots*, Buzzfeed News, Dec. 5, 2018, https://www.buzzfeednews.com/article/briannasacks/dowless-britt-inside-north-carolina-absentee-ballot-machine [https://perma.cc/NGD9–8RUN].

13. Alex Daugherty, *Trump, Scott and Rubio Continue to Push Claims of Florida Voter Fraud without Evidence*, Miami Herald, Nov. 12, 2018, https://www.miamiherald.com/news/politics-government/article221528685.html; Colby Itkowitz, *Paul Ryan Isn't Saying There Was Voter Fraud in California. But . . .*, Wash. Post, Nov. 29, 2018, https://www.washingtonpost.com/politics/2018/11/29/paul-ryan-isnt-saying-there-was-voter-fraud-california/.

14. Richard L. Hasen, *Vote Suppressors Unleashed*, Slate, Nov. 27, 2017, https://slate.com/news-and-politics/2017/11/donald-trump-will-supercharge-voter-suppression-if-the-rnc-consent-decree-falls.html; Josh Gerstein, *Judge Ends Consent Decree Limiting RNC "Ballot Security" Activities*, Politico, Jan. 9, 2018, https://www.politico.com/story/2018/01/09/rnc-ballot-security-consent-decree-328995.

15. Bush v. Gore, 531 U.S. 98 (2000). For an extensive examination, see Richard L. Hasen, *The Voting Wars: From Florida 2000 to the Next Election Meltdown*, ch. 2 (2012).

Chapter 1. The Icicle

1. The trial court's decision is Fish v. Kobach, 309 F. Supp. 3d 1048 (D. Kan. 2018). The exchange between Dr. Richman and Dale Ho appears on pages 1600–1601 of the trial transcript, for Mar. 13, 2018, posted at: https://www.aclu.org/other/fish-v-kobach-transcript-day-6-am-0. [https://perma.cc/YT82-J7K7]. On the 30,000-person figure, see *Fish*, 309 F. Supp. 3d at 1073–74, 1111 (noting that sixteen thousand voter registrations had been canceled and thirteen thousand placed on the suspense list at the time of the court's preliminary injunction).

2. On the "fraudulent fraud squad," see Richard L. Hasen, *The Voting Wars: From Florida 2000 to the Next Election Meltdown*, 41–73 (2012). Hunter Woodall, *Kris Kobach Agrees with Donald Trump That "Millions" Voted Illegally but Offers No Evidence*, Kansas City Star, Nov. 30, 2016, 12:18 p.m., https://www.kansascity.com/news/politics-government/article117957143.html. "Of those [supposed 3 to 5 million fraudulent] votes cast, none of 'em come to me. None of 'em come to me. They would all

be for the other side. None of 'em come to me." Aaron Blake, *Donald Trump Claims None of Those 3 to 5 Million Illegal Votes Were Cast for Him. Zero*, Wash. Post, Jan. 26, 2017, https://www.washingtonpost.com/news/the-fix/wp/2017/01/25/donald-trump-claims-none-of-those-3-to-5-million-illegal-votes-were-cast-for-him-zero/?utm_term=.4119d7e8a308.

3. *Fish*, 309 F. Supp. 3d at 1118–19; Fish v. Kobach, 294 F. Supp. 3d 1154 (D. Kan. 2018); Tim Carpenter, *SOS Kris Kobach's Office Paid $1,000 Fine in Federal Case with State-Issued Credit Card*, Topeka Capital-Journal, June 8, 2018, https://www.cjonline.com/news/20180608/sos-kris-kobachs-office-paid-1000-fine-in-federal-case-with-state-issued-credit-card; Tim Carpenter, *Kansas Drops Kris Kobach's Appeal of Contempt Ruling, ACLU Accepts $20,000 in Legal Fees*, Topeka Capital-Journal, Jan. 30, 2019, https://www.cjonline.com/news/20190129/kansas-drops-kris-kobachs-appeal-of-contempt-ruling-aclu-accepts-20000-for-legal-fees.

4. For an introduction to Hans von Spakovsky, see *Voting Wars, supra* note 2, at 62–63. Judge Robinson's biography is posted at http://ksd.uscourts.gov/index.php/judge/julie-a-robinson/ [https://perma.cc/C73C-RDWX].

5. 52 U.S.C. § 20504(c)(2)(B)-(C) (2018); see *Fish*, 309 F. Supp. 3d at 1097–98.

6. Fish v. Kobach, 840 F.3d 710, 738–739 (10th Cir. 2018); Fish v. Kobach, 294 F. Supp. 3d 1048, 1099 (D. Kan. 2018).

7. "The likely percent of non-citizen voters in recent US elections is 0." Stephen Ansolabehere, Samantha Luks, & Brian F. Schaffner, *The Perils of Cherry Picking Low Frequency Events in Large Sample Surveys*, 40 Electoral Stud. 409, 409 (2015) News21, Election Fraud in America, https://votingrights.news21.com/interactive/election-fraud-database/ [https://perma.cc/PP9E-QBD7]. The last prominent investigation into potential large-scale noncitizen voting involved a 1996 Orange County, California, congressional race between Bob Dornan and Loretta Sanchez. The evidence was highly contested. Professor Minnite describes the contested use of federal government data to establish that voters were not citizens, and documents that at least some cases of noncitizen voting involved confusion about eligibility rather than intentional fraud. See Lorraine Minnite, *The Myth of Voter Fraud*, 49–56 (2010). On Kobach's prosecutions, see Ben Strauss, *"Kris Kobach Came After Me for an Honest Mistake,"* Politico, May 21, 2017, https://www.politico.com/magazine/story/2017/05/21/kris-kobach-voter-fraud-investigation-prosecution-215164. On Kobach's single conviction for noncitizen voting, see *Fish*, 309 F. Supp. 3d at 1095.

8. Jesse T. Richman, Gulshan A. Chattha, & David C. Earnest, *Do Non-Citizens Vote in U.S. Elections?*, 36 Electoral Stud. 149, 152–54 (2014).

9. *Fish*, 309 F. Supp. 3d at 1087 ("After extrapolating the CCES survey results of 4 out of 14 noncitizen registrations to an estimated noncitizen adult population in Kansas of 114,000, Dr. Richman estimated that 28.5%, or 32,000 noncitizens, were registered to vote, with a confidence interval of between 11.7% and 54.6%.").

10. Ansolabehere, Luks, & Schaffner, *supra* note 7, at 409; *Fish*, 309 F. Supp. 3d at 1087. A copy of the open letter is posted at: https://www.courthousenews.com/wp-content/uploads/2018/03/Kansas-Voter-ID-LETTER.pdf [https://perma.cc/G64H-XZ2W].

11. *Fish*, 309 F. Supp. 3d at 1092–93.

12. See Mar. 13, 2018, trial transcript, *supra* note 1, at 1060–63.

13. Dale Ho's cross-examination of von Spakovsky appears on pp. 1093–1170 of the trial transcript, for Mar. 9, 2018, posted at: https://www.aclu.org/other/fish-v-kobach-transcript-day-4-pm [https://perma.cc/QKS6-HZH4]. The specific points in the paragraph are referenced on pp. 1094, 1097, 1107–9, 1137, and 1121.

14. Voter impersonation fraud made up 0.5 percent (or ten cases of over two thousand) in the News21 database, https://votingrights.news21.com/interactive/election-fraud-database/ [https://perma.cc/PP9E-QBD7]. Professor Levitt described his research in Justin Levitt, *A Comprehensive Investigation of Voter Impersonation Finds 31 Credible Incidents out of One Billion Votes Cast*, Wash. Post, Wonkblog, Aug. 6, 2014, https://www.washingtonpost.com/news/wonk/wp/2014/08/06/a-comprehensive-investigation-of-voter-impersonation-finds-31-credible-incidents-out-of-one-billion-ballots-cast/. Since I wrote my 2012 book, Levitt flagged two possible organized attempts at impersonation fraud, both in local elections in ultra-Orthodox Jewish communities. For details on these cases, see Max Rivlin-Nadler et al., *Brazen Voting Fraud Alleged among Ultra-Orthodox in Williamsburg*, Gothamist, Sept. 11, 2013, http://gothamist.com/2013/09/11/voter_fraud_attempts.php [https://perma.cc/V2FD-XGKH]; Chris McKenna, *Inside the Kiryas Joel Voting Machine*, Times Herald-Record, Oct. 26, 2014, https://www.recordonline.com/article/20141026/NEWS/141029573.

15. *Voting Wars*, *supra* note 2, at 63; Jane Mayer, *The Voter-Fraud Myth*, New Yorker, Oct. 29 & Nov. 5, 2012, https://www.newyorker.com/magazine/2012/10/29/the-voter-fraud-myth.

16. Mar. 9, 2018, trial transcript, *supra* note 13, at 1159–60. See the Editor's Note from Nov. 12, 2018, accompanying a 2012 report, Gary Fineout, *2012 Election: Nearly 200,000 Florida Voters May Not Be Citizens*, NBC Miami, May 11, 2012, https://www.nbcmiami.com/news/local/Nearly-200000-Florida-Voters-May-Not-Be-Citizens-151212725.html [https://perma.cc/SAS2-73JD].

17. Mar. 9, 2018, trial transcript, *supra* note 13, at 1166–68.

18. Rick Hasen, *More Hans v. Reality*, Election Law Blog, July 28, 2011, http://electionlawblog.org/?p=20953 [https://perma.cc/7MD3-KZV4]; Rick Hasen, *I Guess von Spakovsky Reads My Blog*, Election Law Blog, July 28, 2011, http://electionlawblog.org/?p=21016 [https://perma.cc/9U5Z-PYA4]. A variation of this paragraph first appeared in my book *The Voting Wars, supra* note 2, at 64.

19. Mar. 9, 2018, trial transcript, *supra* note 13, at 1157–58, 1188.

20. *Fish*, 309 F. Supp. 3d at 1109–10.

21. *Id.* at 1108–9.

22. *Id.* at 1103.

23. Jessica Huseman, *Trump's Voter Fraud Commission Is Gone, But Scrutiny Will Continue*, ProPublica, Jan. 4, 2018, https://www.propublica.org/article/trump-voter-fraud-commission-is-gone-but-scrutiny-will-continue [https://perma.cc/V9GG-YH7W].

24. Richard L. Hasen, *Trump's Voting Investigation Is a Great Idea; As Long as It Looks Like This*, Slate, Jan. 25, 2017, https://slate.com/news-and-politics/2017/01/trumps-voting-fraud-investigation-is-a-great-idea.html.

25. The commission's report, supplemental materials, and the biographies of its members are available at https://bipartisanpolicy.org/the-presidential-commission-on-election-administration/ [https://perma.cc/8ENX-GQBV]. See also Rick Hasen, *Breaking: Bauer-Ginsberg Election Reform Commission Names Members, Appoints Nate Persily as Sr. Research Director*, Election Law Blog, May 21, 2013, https://electionlawblog.org/?p=50792 [https://perma.cc/G46Q-M255] for a list of original leadership, including Mr. Britton and Professor Persily.

26. Rick Hasen, *Report of Presidential Commission on Electoral Administration Appears Gone*, Election Law Blog, Jan. 27, 2017, http://electionlawblog.org/?p=90741 [https://perma.cc/T645-XDJS]; Rick Hasen, *Breaking: Trump to Launch a Voting "Commission" with No Credibility, with Pence, Kobach, and the EAC's McCormick*, Election Law Blog, May 11, 2017, https://electionlawblog.org/?p=92471 [https://perma.cc/WX3E-B4LM]; Rick Hasen, *Kobach Relies on "Bipartisan" Nature of Election Commission for Legitimacy, but It Is Hardly Bipartisan*, Election Law Blog, July 4, 2017, 5:11 p.m., https://electionlawblog.org/?p=93553 [https://perma.cc/A96A-CVXZ].

27. @LawyersComm, Twitter, July 11, 2017, 1:51 p.m. PST, https://twitter.com/LawyersComm/status/884877749151817728 [https://perma.cc/C73T-DJA5] ("American Horror Story: Trump Edition Four Horsemen of Voter Suppression named for Sham Election Integrity Commission. #ProtectMyVote").

28. Tierney Sneed, *Ex-Trump Voter Fraud Commissioner Settles Lawsuit Over "Alien Invasion" Reports*, Talking Points Memo, July 17, 2019, https://talkingpointsmemo. com/muckraker/trump-voter-fraud-comissioner-defamation-lawsuit-settled [https:// perma.cc/75ZG-8N3Z]; Ben Jacobs, *Controversial Rightwing Activist to Join Trump's Election Integrity Commission*, Guardian, July 11, 2017, https://www.theguardian.com/ us-news/2017/jul/11/trump-election-integrity-commission-j-christian-adams [https:// perma.cc/746Z-DFMN]; Jane C. Timm, *Voter Fraud Crusader J. Christian Adams Sparks Outrage*, NBC News, Aug. 27, 2017, https://www.nbcnews.com/politics/ donald-trump/vote-fraud-crusader-j-christian-adams-sparks-outrage-n796026; Peter Galuszka, *An Alien Invasion in the Old Dominion?* Wash. Post, Oct. 6, 2016, https:// www.washingtonpost.com/blogs/all-opinions-are-local/wp/2016/10/06/an-alien-invasion-in-the-old-dominion/ ("Arriving just in time for the Nov. 8 elections is a 'report' whose cover features a 1950s-style flying saucer approaching bucolic Virginia"); *Voting Wars, supra* note 2, at 120; David Folkenflik, *Conservative Media Stokes New Black Panther Story*, NPR, July 20, 2010, https://www.npr.org/templates/story/story. php?storyId=128647537 [https://perma.cc/L84K-LZR3].

29. Tierney Sneed, *Discovery Dispute Surfaces Emails between Ex Trump Voter Fraud Commissioners*, Talking Points Memo, Mar. 1, 2019, https://talkingpointsmemo.com/ muckraker/christian-adams-von-spakovsky-emails-pilf-lulac-lawsuit [https://perma. cc/GDG5-MR5V]; Rick Hasen, *"Push His Buttons": J. Christian Adams Calls Me "Raw Enemy Activist," Plots with Von Spakovsky, PILF Employees to Counter My Calling Out the Work of the Fraudulent Fraud Squad*, Election Law Blog, Mar. 1, 2019, https:// electionlawblog.org/?p=103840 [https://perma.cc/WCL5-D2UF].

30. *Bill Gardner Hangs On as N.H. Secretary of State by Slimmest of Margins*, NHPR, Dec. 5, 2018, https://www.nhpr.org/post/bill-gardner-hangs-nh-secretary-state-slimmest-margins#stream/0; Richard L. Hasen, *Commentary: Dunlap Badly Mistaken in Agreeing to Serve on Trump Voter Fraud Panel*, Portland Press Herald, May 24, 2017, https://www.pressherald.com/2017/05/24/commentary-dunlap-badly-mistaken-in-agreeing-to-serve-on-trump-voter-fraud-panel/.

31. Rick Hasen, *Updated: Someone at Heritage Sent Letter Urging Pence-Kobach to Keep Democrats, Mainstream Republicans, and Academics off Fraud Commission*, Election Law Blog, Sept. 12, 2017, https://electionlawblog.org/?p=94768 [https://perma. cc/M5LN-4CW9]; Hunter Woodall, *Email from Key Player on Kobach-Led Voter Fraud Commission: Keep Democrats off Panel*, Kansas City Star, Sept. 13, 2017, https:// www.kansascity.com/news/politics-government/article173178756.html.

32. Roxana Hegeman, *Lawsuit Claims Kansas Official Exposed Private Voter Data*, Associated Press, June 19, 2018, https://www.apnews.com/8bdb79714d604e04a296d91 5e37f77ab [https://perma.cc/QV33-R3S3]; Office of the Secretary of State, "Secretary of State Alex Padilla Responds to Presidential Election Commission Request for Personal Data of California Voters," news release number AP17:042, June 29, 2017, https://www.sos.ca.gov/administration/news-releases-and-advisories/2017-news-releases-and-advisories/secretary-state-alex-padilla-responds-presidential-election-commission-request-personal-data-california-voters/ [https://perma.cc/QCV6-WECJ].

33. Brooke Seipel, *Mississippi Official: Fraud Commission Can "Go Jump in Gulf of Mexico,"* The Hill, June 30, 2017, https://thehill.com/blogs/blog-briefing-room/news/340307-miss-official-on-trump-voter-fraud-request-they-can-go-jump-in; Adam Ganuchaeu, *Hosemann on Trump Voter ID Request: "Go Jump in the Gulf,"* Mississippi Today, June 30, 2017, https://mississippitoday.org/2017/06/30/hosemann-on-trump-voter-id-request-go-jump-in-the-gulf/; Jessica Huseman, *Election Commission Documents Cast Doubt on Trump's Claims of Voter Fraud*, ProPublica, Aug. 3, 2018, https://www.propublica.org/article/election-commission-documents-cast-doubt-on-trumps-claims-of-voter-fraud [https://perma.cc/59TS-KG7A].

34. Allison Kite, *Data Collected by Trump's Kobach-Led Voter Fraud Commission Is "Entirely Deleted,"* Kansas City Star, Aug. 30, 2018, https://www.kansascity.com/news/politics-government/article217593970.html; Brennan Center, *Legal Actions Taken Against Trump's "Voter Fraud" Commission*, Dec. 26, 2017, https://www.brennancenter.org/legal-actions-taken-against-trump%E2%80%99s-%E2%80%9Cfraud%E2%80%9D-commission [https://perma.cc/XC7B-BPVW].

35. Eli Watkins, *Judge Sides with Dem Member Suing Trump Voting Commission*, CNN, Dec. 25, 2017, https://www.cnn.com/2017/12/24/politics/matthew-dunlap-voter-fraud-commission/index.html; Huseman, *supra* note 33. The June 22, 2017, letter with von Spakovsky's and Adams's suggestions for the voter registration information to request from states is posted at https://www.documentcloud.org/documents/4635501-PRODoo1-0005992.html#document/p353/a444757 [https://perma.cc/7SCR-ZVZY].

36. *Kris Kobach on What Led to the Disbandment of Controversial Election Commission*, NPR, Jan. 4, 2018, https://www.npr.org/2018/01/04/575774092/kris-kobach-on-what-led-to-the-disbandment-of-controversial-election-commission; Franco Ordoñez & Bryan Lowry, *Contrary to His Claims, Kobach Not Part of New Voter Fraud Investigation, DHS Says*, Kansas City Star, Jan. 18, 2018, https://www.kansascity.com/news/politics-government/article193647529.html; John Binder, *Exclusive—Kris*

Kobach: Voter Fraud Commission "Being Handed off" to DHS, Will No Longer Be "Stone-walled" by Dems, Breitbart, Jan. 3, 2018, https://www.breitbart.com/politics/2018/01/03/exclusive-kris-kobach-voter-fraud-commission-being-handed-off-to-dhs-will-no-longer-be-stonewalled-by-dems/ [https://perma.cc/Y2ED-JFZM]; Office of the Press Secretary, "Statement by the Press Secretary on the Presidential Advisory Commission on Election Integrity," The White House, Jan. 3, 2018, https://www.whitehouse.gov/briefings-statements/statement-press-secretary-presidential-advisory-commission-election-integrity/ [https://perma.cc/QRL7–4RVB]; @realdonaldtrump, Twitter, Jan. 4, 2018, 3:02 a.m. PST, https://twitter.com/realDonaldTrump/status/948872192284155904 [https://perma.cc/4UD3-T3TY] ("Many mostly Democrat States refused to hand over data from the 2016 Election to the Commission on Voter Fraud. They fought hard that the Commission not see their records or methods because they know that many people are voting illegally. System is rigged, must go to Voter I.D."); Elizabeth Landers, Eli Watkins, & Kevin Liptak, *Trump Dissolves Voter Fraud Commission; Adviser Says It Went "Off the Rails,"* CNN, Jan. 4, 2018, https://www.cnn.com/2018/01/03/politics/presidential-election-commission/index.html; John DiStaso, *NH Primary Source: Kobach Walks Back NH Voter Fraud "Proof" Claim*, WMUR, Sept. 14, 2017, https://www.wmur.com/article/nh-primary-source-kobach-walks-back-nh-voter-fraud-proof-claim/12239428 [https://perma.cc/RH48-PV6L].

37. Landers, Watkins, & Liptak, *supra* note 36; Huseman, *supra* note 33; @Elect-Project, Twitter, Jan. 11, 2018, 4:09 p.m. PST, https://twitter.com/electproject/status/951607020498677761 [https://perma.cc/4UM9-YF79] ("A staffer in Pence's office was quoted as saying working with Kobach was a shit sandwich. Maybe that quote wasn't actually from a staffer . . .").

38. NPR, *supra* note 36.

39. Carpenter, *supra* note 3; Caroline Kenny, *Photo of Trump-Kobach Meeting Reveals Apparent DHS Proposal*, CNN, Nov. 21, 2016, https://www.cnn.com/2016/11/21/politics/kris-kobach-donald-trump-department-of-homeland-security/index.html; Orion Danjuma, *Unsealed Documents Show That Kris Kobach Is Dead Set on Suppressing the Right to Vote*, ACLU Blog, Oct. 26, 2017, https://www.aclu.org/blog/voting-rights/fighting-voter-suppression/unsealed-documents-show-kris-kobach-dead-set (comparing ACLU brief with language Kobach proposed for amending NVRA) [https://perma.cc/KL6X-TW4M]. The unredacted portion of Kobach's draft document mentioning the NVRA amendment is available at https://www.aclu.org/sites/default/files/field_document/fish_v_kobach_exhibit_u.pdf [https://perma.cc/5Q9A-3ACA].

40. Brennan Center for Justice, *New Voting Restrictions in America*, https://www.brennancenter.org/new-voting-restrictions-america (last visited Mar. 1, 2019) [https://perma.cc/VHZ3-WLCP].

41. According to U.S. Census figures for 2018, whites made up 70.8 percent of North Carolina's population, African Americans 22.2 percent, and Hispanics (who can be of any race) 9.5 percent. https://www.census.gov/quickfacts/nc [https://perma.cc/9NLY-FDRT]. A Department of Justice website lists the North Carolina counties that were covered by the Section 5 preclearance rules until 2013: https://www.justice.gov/crt/jurisdictions-previously-covered-section-5 [https://perma.cc/3SAF-E5GA]. As the website also explains: "Under Section 5, any change with respect to voting in a covered jurisdiction—or any political subunit within it—cannot legally be enforced unless and until the jurisdiction first obtains the requisite determination by the United States District Court for the District of Columbia or makes a submission to the Attorney General. This requires proof that the proposed voting change does not deny or abridge the right to vote on account of race, color, or membership in a language minority group. If the jurisdiction is unable to prove the absence of such discrimination, the District Court denies the requested judgment, or in the case of administrative submissions, the Attorney General objects to the change, and it remains legally unenforceable." U.S. Department of Justice, *About Section 5 of the Voting Rights Act*, https://www.justice.gov/crt/about-section-5-voting-rights-act [https://perma.cc/2GEZ-7WXQ].

42. Shelby County v. Holder, 570 U.S. 529, 540, 544 (2013); *id.* at 590 (Ginsburg, J. dissenting); Leah Litman, *Inventing Equal Sovereignty*, 114 Mich. L. Rev. 1207 (2016).

43. *For Republicans, No Easy Answers on Voting Rights Act*, Associated Press, July 5, 2013, https://www.cbsnews.com/news/for-republicans-no-easy-answers-on-voting-rights-act/ ("GOP officials in Texas and Mississippi promised within hours of the decision to enforce new laws requiring voters to show identification at polls."); Rebecca Leber, *In Texas You Can Vote with a Concealed Handgun License—But Not a Student ID*, New Republic, Oct. 20, 2014, https://newrepublic.com/article/119900/texas-voter-id-allows-handgun-licenses-not-student-ids.

44. For the text of the law, see H.B. 589, 2013 Gen. Assemb., Reg. Sess. (N.C. 2013), available at http://www.ncga.state.nc.us/Sessions/2013/Bills/House/PDF/H589v8.pdf [https://perma.cc/P44H-VRNH]; see also Evan Perez, *Justice Department Sues North Carolina over Voting Law*, CNN, Sept. 30, 2013, 6:01 p.m., http://www.cnn.com/2013/09/30/us/north-carolina-voting-lawsuit. This paragraph draws from Richard L. Hasen, *Race or Party?: How Courts Should Think about Republican*

Efforts to Make It Harder to Vote in North Carolina and Elsewhere, 127 Harv. L. Rev. F. 58 (2014), https://harvardlawreview.org/2014/01/race-or-party-how-courts-should-think-about-republican-efforts-to-make-it-harder-to-vote-in-north-carolina-and-elsewhere/.

45. The next few paragraphs draw from Richard L. Hasen, *Race or Party, Race as Party, or Party All the Time: Three Uneasy Approaches to Conjoined Polarization in Redistricting and Voting Cases*, 59 Wm. & Mary L. Rev. 1837 (2018); N.C. State Conf. of NAACP v. McCrory, 182 F. Supp. 3d 320, 498 (M.D.N.C. 2016), *rev'd*, 831 F.3d 204 (4th Cir. 2016), *cert. denied*, 137 S. Ct. 1399 (2017).

46. N.C. State Conference of NAACP v. McCrory, 831 F.3d 204, 214 (4th Cir. 2016), *cert. denied*, 137 S. Ct. 1399 (2017).

47. *Id.* at 228, 233.

48. Richard L. Hasen, *There's a Simple Step North Carolina's New Governor Could Take to Strengthen Voting Rights*, Slate, Feb. 2, 2017, https://slate.com/news-and-politics/2017/02/north-carolina-should-withdraw-its-petition-to-the-supreme-court-in-its-voting-rights-case.html; Vann R. Newkirk II, *North Carolina's Voter ID Law Is Defeated, for Now*, Atlantic, May 15, 2017, https://www.theatlantic.com/politics/archive/2017/05/north-carolinas-voter-id-law-supreme-court-cert/526713/; North Carolina v. North Carolina State Conference of the NAACP, 137 S. Ct. 1399, 1400 (2017) (statement of Roberts, C. J., respecting the denial of certiorari) ("Given the blizzard of filings over who is and who is not authorized to seek review in this Court under North Carolina law, it is important to recall our frequent admonition that '[t]he denial of a writ of certiorari imports no expression of opinion upon the merits of the case.'").

49. Anne Blythe, *4th U.S. Circuit Judges Overturn North Carolina's Voter ID Law*, Charlotte Observer, July 30, 2016, https://www.charlotteobserver.com/news/politics-government/article92595012.html; Judge Schroeder's biography is posted on the Federal Judicial Center website at https://www.fjc.gov/history/judges/schroeder-thomas-d [https://perma.cc/TF9K-CUE7]. Husted v. A. Philip Randolph Institute, 138 S. Ct. 1833 (2018); Crawford v. Marion Cy. Elect. Bd., 553 U.S. 181 (2008).

50. Lynn Bonner, *Voter ID Becomes Law in North Carolina as House Overrides Veto*, News & Observer, Dec. 19, 2018, https://www.newsobserver.com/news/politics-government/article223310620.html; Will Doran, *Democrat Anita Earls Claims Victory in NC Supreme Court Race*, News & Observer, Nov. 6, 2018, https://www.newsobserver.com/news/politics-government/article221037190.html.

51. According to the U.S. Census, whites made up about 86 percent of Kansas's population in 2018. https://www.census.gov/quickfacts/ks [https://perma.cc/2R7

6-Q5M8]. Whites made up just under 86 percent of Indiana's population in 2018. U.S. Census Bureau, *Quick Facts: Indiana,* https://www.census.gov/quickfacts/fact/table/in/PST045218 [https://perma.cc/A464-758R]. Crawford v. Marion Cty. Elec. Bd, 553 U.S. 181 (2008).

52. "Despite apocalyptic assertions of wholesale voter disenfranchisement, Plaintiffs have produced not a single piece of evidence of any identifiable registered voter who would be prevented from voting pursuant to [the law] because of his or her inability to obtain the necessary photo identification. Similarly, Plaintiffs have failed to produce any evidence of any individual, registered or unregistered, who would have to obtain photo identification in order to vote, let alone anyone who would undergo any appreciable hardship to obtain photo identification in order to be qualified to vote." Indiana Dem. Party v. Rokita, 458 F. Supp. 2d 775, 822–23 (S.D. Ind. 2006), *aff'd sub. nom* Crawford v. Marion County Election Bd., 472 F.3d 949, 951 (7th Cir. 2007), *aff'd,* 553 U.S. 181 (2008). *Judge Sarah Evans Barker to Step Back on Duties,* Indy Star, Mar. 31, 2014, https://www.indystar.com/story/news/2014/03/31/judge-sarah-evans-barker-step-back-duties/7136267/.

53. Posner wrote: "A great many people who are eligible to vote don't bother to do so. Many do not register, and many who do register still don't vote, or vote infrequently. The benefits of voting to the individual voter are elusive (a vote in a political election rarely has any *instrumental* value, since elections for political office at the state or federal level are never decided by just one vote), and even very slight costs in time or bother or out-of-pocket expense deter many people from voting, or at least from voting in elections they're not much interested in. So some people who have not bothered to obtain a photo ID will not bother to do so just to be allowed to vote, and a few who have a photo ID but forget to bring it to the polling place will say what the hell and not vote, rather than go home and get the ID and return to the polling place." Crawford v. Marion County Election Bd., 472 F.3d 949, 951 (7th Cir. 2007), *aff'd,* 553 U.S. 181 (2008). See also *id.* at 954 (7th Cir. 2007) (dissenting opinion).

54. This discussion of *Crawford* draws in part from *Voting Wars, supra* note 2, at 81–88.

55. Richard A. Posner, *Reflections on Judging,* 84–85 (2013).

56. On the lack of a connection between voter identification laws and public confidence in the integrity of the election system, see Stephen Ansolabehere & Nathaniel Persily, *Vote Fraud in the Eye of the Beholder: The Role of Public Opinion in the Challenge to Voter Identification Requirements,* 121 Harv. L. Rev. 1737 (2008).

57. *Crawford*, 553 U.S. at 184–204 (Stevens, J., plurality opinion); *id.* at 204–9 (Scalia, J., concurring in the judgment).

58. Enrico Cantoni & Vincent Pons, *Strict ID Laws Don't Stop Voters: Evidence from a U.S. Nationwide Panel, 2008–2016* (Nat'l Bureau of Econ. Research Working Paper No. 25522, Feb. 2019, https://www.nber.org/papers/w25522; Jacob R. Neiheisel & Rich Horner, *Voter Identification Requirements and Aggregate Turnout in the U.S.: How Campaigns Offset the Costs of Turning Out When Voting Is Made More Difficult*, Election L.J. (forthcoming), https://www.liebertpub.com/doi/abs/10.1089/elj.2018.0500.

59. Roey Hadar, *North Dakota Reservations See Record Voter Turnout amid Fears of Suppression*, ABC News, Nov. 7, 2018, https://abcnews.go.com/Politics/north-dakota-reservations-record-voter-turnout-amid-fears/story?id=59038845; Carrie Levine, *Backlash over North Dakota Voter ID Law Could Rally Native Americans*, Center for Public Integrity, Nov. 1, 2018, https://publicintegrity.org/federal-politics/backlash-over-north-dakota-voter-id-law-could-rally-native-americans/ [https://perma.cc/NB3A-ZPUQ]; Maggie Astor, *In North Dakota, Native Americans Try to Turn an ID Law to Their Advantage*, N.Y. Times, Oct. 30, 2018, https://www.nytimes.com/2018/10/30/us/politics/north-dakota-voter-id.html.

60. On the problems with "softening" voter identification laws, see Richard L. Hasen, *Softening Voter ID Laws through Litigation: Is it Enough?* 2016 Wis. L. Rev. Forward 100 (2016), http://wisconsinlawreview.org/wp-content/uploads/2016/09/Hasen-Final.pdf [https://perma.cc/RE87-3WF5].

61. Jim Malewitz, *After Early Voting Glitches, Officials Hope New Texas Voter ID Rules Are Clear*, Texas Tribune, Nov. 7, 2016, https://www.keranews.org/post/after-early-voting-glitches-officials-hope-new-texas-voter-id-rules-are-clear; Kira Lerner, *The Powerful Role Confusion Plays in American Elections*, Talking Points Memo, Dec. 28, 2018, https://talkingpointsmemo.com/feature/the-powerful-role-confusion-plays-in-american-elections [https://perma.cc/AS68-SBAM]; Tim Reid & Grant Smith, *Missing Hyphens Will Make It Harder for Some People to Vote in U.S. Election*, Reuters, Apr. 11, 2018, https://www.reuters.com/article/us-usa-election-laws/missing-hyphens-will-make-it-hard-for-some-people-to-vote-in-u-s-election-idUSKBN1HI1PX [https://perma.cc/BJ4W-GKBL].

62. Ari Berman, *Wisconsin Is Systematically Failing to Provide the Photo IDs Required to Vote in November*, Nation, Sept. 29, 2016, https://www.thenation.com/article/wisconsin-is-systematically-failing-to-provide-the-photo-ids-required-to-vote-in-november/; Patrick Marley, *Judge Blasts State over Voter ID*, Milwaukee

Journal Sentinel, Oct. 12, 2016, https://www.jsonline.com/story/news/politics/
elections/2016/10/12/judge-blasts-state-over-voter-id/91939226/.

63. Tom Kerstcher, *Hillary Clinton's Claim in Her New Book about Voter Suppression in Wisconsin*, PolitiFact, Sept. 12, 2017, https://www.politifact.com/wisconsin/
article/2017/sep/12/hillary-clintons-claim-her-new-book-about-voter-su/ [https://
perma.cc/9VNH-UQT9]; Tom Kerstcher, *Hillary Clinton's Mostly False Claim on
Photo ID, Voter Suppression in Wisconsin in 2016 Election*, PolitiFact, June 9, 2017,
https://www.politifact.com/wisconsin/statements/2017/jun/09/hillary-clinton/
hillary-clintons-mostly-false-claim-photo-id-voter/ [https://perma.cc/MNX5-
V3PG]. One controversial study released after Clinton made her remarks found that
up to seventeen thousand voters (not two hundred thousand as Clinton claimed)
were kept from the polls in the 2016 presidential race in Wisconsin because of the
state's voter identification law. Michael Wines, *Wisconsin Strict ID Law Discouraged
Voters, Study Finds*, N.Y. Times, Sept. 25, 2017, https://www.nytimes.com/2017/09/25/
us/wisconsin-voters.html (quoting the study's author, Professor Kenneth Mayer, as
stating: "The survey did not ask any questions about how people would have voted or
about their party identification. . . . But it's certainly possible that there were enough
voters deterred that it flipped the election."). The study's findings and data are posted
at Elections Research Center at the University of Wisconsin–Madison, *Voter ID
Study*, https://elections.wisc.edu/voter-id-study/ [https://perma.cc/7LPV-J9U9]. On
the controversy surrounding the study, see Lisa Speckhard Pasque, *UW Prof. Defends
His Study That Found Voter ID Law Deterred Thousands from Voting*, Cap. Times, Dec.
18, 2017, https://madison.com/ct/news/local/govt-and-politics/uw-prof-defends-his-
study-that-found-voter-id-law/article_b105292f-2dc9-55f4-948e-fffd18dbcdc6.html;
Bill Glauber, *Hillary Clinton Was Caught by Surprise by Wisconsin Loss, She Says in
Her Book, "What Happened,"* Milwaukee Journal Sentinel, Sept. 12, 2017, https://
www.jsonline.com/story/news/2017/09/12/hillary-clinton-discusses-wisconsin-loss-
herds-book-lands-wisconsin-filled-explanations-her-loss-her/657485001/ [https://
perma.cc/6LVL-A55M].

64. On the difficulty of tying voter identification laws to turnout, see Robert S.
Erickson & Lorraine C. Minnite, *Modeling Problems in the Voter Identification—Voter
Turnout Debate*, 8 Election L.J. 85, 98 (2009) ("We should be wary of claims—from
all sides of the controversy—regarding turnout effects from voter ID laws. . . . The
data are not up to the task of making a compelling statistical argument."). On how
voter identification laws especially burden minority voters, see Zoltan Hajnal, Nazita
Lajevardi, & Lindsay Nielson, *Voter Identification Laws and the Suppression of Minority*

Votes, 79 J. Pol. 363 (2017). For a recent broad study finding that that voter ID laws appear to prevent no fraud and deter no turnout, see Cantoni & Pons, *supra* note 58.

65. Alexa Ura, *"Someone Did Not Do Their Due Diligence": How an Attempt to Review Texas' Voter Rolls Turned into a Debacle*, Texas Tribune, Feb. 1, 2019, https://www.texastribune.org/2019/02/01/texas-citizenship-voter-roll-review-how-it-turned-boondoggle/; Roque Planas, *Latino Turnout Surged. Then Texas Questioned 98,000 Voters' Citizenship*, HuffPost, Jan. 29, 2019, https://www.huffingtonpost.com/entry/latino-turnout-surged-then-texas-challenged-98000-voters-citizenship_us_5c50cbc4e4b00906b26e490d.

66. Madeline Fox & Scott Canon, *Kobach Steps Aside on Vote Count in GOP Kansas Governor Primary with Colyer*, KCUR, Aug. 10, 2018, https://www.kcur.org/post/kobach-steps-aside-vote-count-gop-kansas-governor-primary-colyer#stream/0.

67. Sherman Smith, *Judge Blocks Release of Video of Kris Kobach Deposition by ACLU*, Topeka Capital-Journal, Oct. 26, 2018, https://www.cjonline.com/news/20181025/judge-blocks-release-of-video-of-kris-kobach-deposition-by-aclu; Bryan Lowry, *Video of Kobach Reveals Details of Private Talks with Trump, Members of Congress*, Kansas City Star, Mar. 9, 2018, https://www.kansascity.com/latest-news/article204461409.html; Maggie Haberman & Annie Karni, *A Would-Be Trump Aide's Demands: A Jet on Call, a Future Cabinet Post and More*, N.Y. Times, May 20, 2019, https://www.nytimes.com/2019/05/20/us/politics/kris-kobach-trump.html.

68. Tim Elfrink, *Voter Registration Groups Sue to Block Tennessee Law with Tough Penalties for Signup Mistakes*, Wash. Post, May 3, 2019, https://www.washingtonpost.com/nation/2019/05/03/voter-registration-groups-sue-block-tennessee-law-with-tough-penalties-signup-mistakes/?utm_term=.06c76e75abe4.

Chapter 2. The Weakest Link

1. *Broward Submits Machine Recount Results 2 Minutes Late, Won't Count Towards Election Total*, CBS Miami/AP, Nov. 15, 2018, https://miami.cbslocal.com/2018/11/15/broward-county-finishes-machine-recount/; Susannah Bryan, *Both Sides Lob Insults as Recount of 700,000 Ballots in Broward Begins*, S. Fla. Sun-Sentinel, Nov. 12, 2018, https://www.sun-sentinel.com/local/broward/fl-ne-florida-recount-sunday-original-20181112-story.html.

2. Nancy Smith, *Snipes Misses Her Deadline by 2 Minutes; It Costs Scott and Caldwell Hundreds of Votes*, Sunshine State News, Nov. 16, 2018, http://sunshinestate-news.com/story/snipes-misses-her-deadline-2-minutes-it-costs-scott-and-caldwell-hundreds-votes.

3. CBS Miami/AP, *supra* note 1; Smith, *supra* note 2.

4. Anthony Man, *Trump Bashes Broward County and Brenda Snipes Over Election Issues*, S. Fla. Sun-Sentinel, Nov. 9, 2018, https://www.sun-sentinel.com/news/politics/fl-ne-florida-voting-ballots-senate-friday-20181109-story.html; David Smith, *Brenda Snipes: How a Florida Election Official Became Focus of Recount Fury*, Guardian, Nov. 15, 2018, https://www.theguardian.com/us-news/2018/nov/15/brenda-snipes-how-a-florida-election-official-became-focus-of-recount-fury.

5. Smith, *supra* note 2; Steve Bosquet & Nicholas Nehamas, *Scott's Request for FDLE Probe of Broward Vote Draws Criticism—and Goes Nowhere*, Tampa Bay Times, Nov. 9, 2018, https://www.tampabay.com/florida-politics/buzz/2018/11/09/scotts-request-for-fdle-probe-of-broward-vote-draws-criticism-and-goes-nowhere/. On Hanlon's Razor in the election administration context, see Richard L. Hasen, *The Voting Wars: From Florida 2000 to the Next Election Meltdown* 7 (2012).

6. Scott Wyman & Jean-Paul Renaud, *Broward to Resend Ballots, Add Workers*, S. Fla. Sun-Sentinel, Oct. 28, 2004, https://www.sun-sentinel.com/news/fl-xpm-2004–10–28–0410280399-story.html.

7. Dan Sweeney, *A Look at Broward Elections Chief Brenda Snipes' Long History of Trouble*, S. Fla. Sun-Sentinel, Nov. 9, 2018, https://www.sun-sentinel.com/news/politics/fl-ne-who-is-brenda-snipes-20181109-story.html.

8. Alex Harris & Martin Vassolo, *Broward to Submit First Vote Tally, Not Flawed Machine Recount, to State on Sunday*, Miami Herald, Nov. 17, 2018, https://www.miamiherald.com/news/politics-government/election/article221829255.html.

9. AP, *Judge Rules in Gov. Scott's Favor, Orders Snipes to Allow Ballot Inspections Immediately*, Nov. 9, 2018, https://www.local10.com/news/elections/emergency-hearing-to-be-held-after-rick-scott-files-lawsuit-against-broward-elections-supervisor.

10. All of these incidents are explored in greater depth in *Voting Wars, supra* note 5, ch. 1. On the history of punch card voting in elections, see Douglas W. Jones, A Brief Illustrated History of Voting, 6, Punched Cards for Voting (2001, updated 2003), http://homepage.cs.uiowa.edu/~jones/voting/pictures/#punchcard [https://perma.cc/6378-TXHT].

11. Alexander Gonzalez, *Expert: How Ballot Design Could Impact Broward County Election Results*, WLRN, Nov. 12, 2018, http://www.wlrn.org/post/expert-how-ballot-design-could-impact-broward-county-election-results; Mike Vassilinda, *Broward Ballot Design Could Have Cost Nelson Election*, WFLA, Nov. 19, 2018, https://www.wfla.com/news/florida/broward-ballot-design-could-have-cost-nelson-election/1607461130. The ballot image appears in this tweet: @NewsbySmiley, Twitter, Nov. 8, 2018, 8:34 a.m.

PST, https://twitter.com/NewsbySmiley/status/1060571314749128704 [https://perma. cc/6YPP-NBDL]. The photograph is reprinted with the permission of David Smiley. The new amendment outlawing this form of the ballot appears in Fl. State. 101.051, subd. 9(a)(1)(b) (as amended, 2019). See SB 7066 (Fl. Leg. 2019), lines 526–40, https:// www.myfloridahouse.gov/Sections/Documents/loaddoc.aspx?FileName=_s7066er. DOCX&DocumentType=Bill&BillNumber=7066&Session=2019 [https://perma.cc/ ZHB9-WMJD].

12. Marc Caputo, *Racial Trouble Looms as Snipes Sues over Suspension*, Politico, Dec. 19, 2018, https://www.politico.com/states/florida/story/2018/12/19/racial-trouble-looms-as-snipes-sues-over-suspension-755551. Scott's order suspending Snipes is posted at https://www.flgov.com/wp-content/uploads/2018/11/SLG-BI-ZHUB18113004050.pdf [https://perma.cc/JT6K-BPGU]. Larry Barszewski, *Brenda Snipes Says Gov. DeSantis Let Her Resign with "My Name and My Dignity" Intact*, S. Fla. Sun-Sentinel, Jan. 18, 2019, https://www.sun-sentinel.com/news/politics/fl-ne-desantis-accepts-snipes-resignation-20190118-story.html.

13. The narrative in the next few paragraphs draws on material in *Voting Wars*, *supra* note 5, ch. 1 and the sources cited therein.

14. For a deep and perceptive look at the lawsuits and legal issues in the Florida 2000 recount period, see Howard Gillman, *The Votes That Counted: How the Court Decided the 2000 Presidential Election* (2001).

15. Bush v. Gore, 531 U.S. 98 (2000); David Margolick, *The Path to Florida*, Vanity Fair, Oct. 2004, https://www.vanityfair.com/news/2004/10/florida-election-2000 (" 'Like we used to say in Brooklyn,' [Scalia] is said to have told a colleague, 'it's a piece of shit.' ").

16. Michael J. Hanmer et al., *Losing Fewer Votes: The Impact of Changing Voting Systems on Residual Votes*, 63 Pol. Res. Q. 129 (2010); Charles Stewart III, *Voter Confidence in the 2018 Elections: So Long to the Winner's Effect?* Election Updates, Dec. 19, 2018, https://electionupdates.caltech.edu/2018/12/19/voter-confidence-in-the-2018-election-so-long-to-the-winners-effect/ [https://perma.cc/3JHZ-2WNH].

17. For a discussion of the methodology used in computing these figures, see Richard L. Hasen, *The 2016 U.S. Voting Wars: From Bad to Worse*, 26 Wm. & Mary Bill of Rts. J. 629, 630–31 (2018). For the most updated version of the database, see https:// electionlawblog.org/wp-content/uploads/Election-Litigation-1996–2018.xlsx [https://perma.cc/99TC-GVSZ].

18. On the prior Wisconsin system of election administration, see Daniel P. Tokaji, *America's Top Model: The Wisconsin Government Accountability Board*, 3 U.C. Irvine L. Rev. 575 (2013), https://www.law.uci.edu/lawreview/vol3/no3/tokaji.pdf.

19. On Florida's change to appointment of secretary of state, see *Voting Wars, supra* note 5, at 199–200. On Ertel's resignation, see Jeffrey Schweers, *Florida Secretary of State Mike Ertel Resigns After Halloween Blackface Photos Emerge*, Tallahassee Democrat, January 24, 2019, https://www.tallahassee.com/story/news/2019/01/24/new-secretary-state-ertel-dressed-blackface-halloween-2005/2649161002/.

20. CBS Miami/AP, *supra* note 1.

21. Frances Robles, *Nearly 3,000 Votes Disappeared from Florida's Recount. That's Not Supposed to Happen*, N.Y. Times, Nov. 16, 2018, https://www.nytimes.com/2018/11/16/us/voting-machines-florida.html.

22. Robles, *supra* note 21; Steve Bousquet, *Suspended Elections Chief Susan Bucher Resigns Rather Than Take Fight to GOP-Controlled Senate*, S. Fla. Sun-Sentinel, Jan. 28, 2019, https://www.sun-sentinel.com/local/palm-beach/fl-ne-susan-bucher-resignation-20190128-story.html.

23. Steve Contorno, *Florida's Elections Official Who Allowed Hurricane Michael Survivors to Vote by Email Stands by Decision*, Tampa Bay Times, Dec. 5, 2018, http://www.tampabay.com/florida-politics/buzz/2018/12/05/how-did-floridas-panhandle-pull-off-an-election-after-a-hurricane-a-ground-zero-election-official-explains/; Diane H. Mazur, *The Bullying of America: A Cautionary Tale about Military Voting and Civil-Military Relations*, 4 Election L.J. 105, 111 (2005).

24. Contorno, *supra* note 23; Samantha J. Gross, *Bill Nelson Sues to Block Fax, Email Votes in Bay County from Being Counted*, Miami Herald, Nov. 15, 2018, https://www.miamiherald.com/news/politics-government/election/article221703710.html.

25. @realDonaldTrump, Twitter, Nov. 12, 2018, 4:44 a.m. PST, https://twitter.com/realDonaldTrump/status/1061962869376540672 [https://perma.cc/GT7Q-8MRE].

26. William Cummings, *Trump Slams "Low IQ" Rep. Maxine Waters Who Called for Harassment of White House Officials*, USA Today, June 25, 2018, https://www.usatoday.com/story/news/politics/onpolitics/2018/06/25/maxine-waters-trump-exchange/732505002/; Jessica Kwong, *Donald Trump Attacked Six Black Women in Three Days: "Nasty," "Loser," "Racist Question," and "Stupid Question,"* Newsweek, Nov. 9, 2018, https://www.newsweek.com/donald-trump-attacked-black-women-racist-question-1209872.

27. *The Voting Wars, supra* note 5, preface.

28. Colby Itkowitz, *Paul Ryan Isn't Saying There Was Voter Fraud in California. But . . .*, Wash. Post, Nov. 29, 2018, https://www.washingtonpost.com/politics/2018/11/29/paul-ryan-isnt-saying-there-was-voter-fraud-california/. On the greater use of provisional ballots in counties with larger number of minority voters, see Joshua Field,

Charles Posner, & Anna Chu, *Uncounted Votes: The Racially Discriminatory Effects of Provisional Ballots*, Center for American Progress, Oct. 29, 2014, https://www.americanprogress.org/issues/race/reports/2014/10/29/99886/uncounted-votes/ [https://perma.cc/P58N-WA8N]; Edward B. Foley, *A Big Blue Shift: Measuring an Asymmetrically Increasing Margin of Litigation*, 28 J. L. & Pol. 501 (2013).

29. "Preserving Democracy: What Went Wrong in Ohio," Status Report of the House Judiciary Committee Democratic Staff, Jan. 5, 2005, at 7–8, https://www.scribd.com/document/392909109/Preserving-Democracy-What-Went-Wrong-in-Ohio-Status-Report-of-the-House-Judiciary-Committee-Democratic-Staff-Conyers-2004 [https://perma.cc/ULA9-J6PQ].

30. John W. Fountain, *The 2000 Elections: Missouri; Senator Refuses to Challenge Loss*, N.Y. Times, Nov. 9, 2000, https://www.nytimes.com/2000/11/09/us/the-2000-elections-missouri-senator-refuses-to-challenge-loss.html.

31. This section draws from Hasen, *supra* note 17, at 649–53. Presidential Com'n on Election Admin., The American Voting Experience: Report and Recommendations of the Presidential Commission on Election Administration, Jan. 2014, 62–64, http://web.mit.edu/supportthevoter/www/files/2014/01/Amer-Voting-Exper-final-draft-01-09-14-508.pdf [https://perma.cc/5QQR-VT2B]] ("Perhaps the most dire warning the Commission heard in its investigation of the topics in the Executive Order concerned the impending crisis in voting technology. Well-known to election administrators, if not the public at large, this impending crisis arises from the widespread wearing out of voting machines purchased a decade ago, the lack of any voting machines on the market that meet the current needs of election administrators, a standard-setting process that has broken down, and a certification process for new machines that is costly and time-consuming. In short, jurisdictions do not have the money to purchase new machines, and legal and market constraints prevent the development of machines they would want even if they had the funds.").

32. Philip Bump, *Donald Trump Will Be President Thanks to 80,000 People in Three States*, Wash. Post, Dec. 1, 2016, https://www.washingtonpost.com/news/the-fix/wp/2016/12/01/donald-trump-will-be-president-thanks-to-80000-people-in-three-states/ [https://perma.cc/2Z8L-LGX6]; Chris Cillizza, *Hillary Clinton's Campaign Wants to Make One Thing Very Clear: They Don't Want a Recount*, Wash. Post, Nov. 29, 2016, https://www.washingtonpost.com/news/the-fix/wp/2016/11/29/hillary-clintons-campaign-didnt-want-this-recount-and-doesnt-think-it-will-change-anything/ [https://perma.cc/2PUZ-8BRC]; Eric Geller, *Citing "Reported Hacks," Jill Stein Says She'll File for Recounts in Three States*, Politico, Nov. 23, 2016, http://www.politico.

com/story/2016/11/jill-stein-recount-three-states-election-hacks-231814 [https://
perma.cc/RZ24-CL56]; Matt Rocheleau, *Stein Raises $2.3 Million for Recount Requests
in Three Key States*, Bos. Globe, Nov. 23, 2016, https://www.bostonglobe.com/
metro/2016/11/23/jill-stein-seeks-recount-wisconsin-michigan-and-pennsylvania/
gmziuhamGOjDgYitbQpWSJ/story.html; Scott Bauer, *Stein Still Stands to Benefit
under Losing Recount Effort*, AP, Dec. 5, 2016, https://apnews.com/000b42099c524f06
9ecd71d4065e05ca/stein-still-stands-benefit-under-losing-recount-effort [https://
perma.cc/52ZY-R2RP]; Marc Erik Elias, *Listening and Responding to Calls for an Audit
and Recount*, Medium, Nov. 26, 2016, https://medium.com/@marceelias/listening-
and-responding-to-calls-for-an-audit-and-recount-2a904717ea39 [https://perma.cc/
YCJ6-ECQF].

33. Joseph Ax, *Jill Stein's Recount Bid Is Over*, HuffPost, Dec. 12, 2016, http://www.
huffingtonpost.com/entry/jill-stein-recount-over_us_584f3b71e4b0bd9c3dfe612e
[https://perma.cc/72SM-QZKS]; Mich. Dep't of State, Executive Summary of
Audits Conducted in Detroit and Statewide in Relation to the November 8, 2016
General Election 1 (2017), http://www.michigan.gov/documents/sos/Combined_
Detroit_Audit_Exec_summary_551188_7.pdf [https://perma.cc/D4ZX-QMQJ]; Joel
Rosenblatt, *Michigan Presidential Ballot Recount Ended by Court Ruling*, Bloomberg,
Dec. 7, 2016, https://www.bloomberg.com/news/articles/2016-12-08/michigan-
allowed-by-judge-to-end-recount-sought-by-greens-stein [https://perma.cc/8JLB-
3P68]; *Stealing the Vote: Recount Uncovers Serious Fraud in Detroit*, World Net Daily,
Dec. 8, 2016, https://www.wnd.com/2016/12/recount-uncovers-serious-fraud-in-
detroit/ [https://perma.cc/2QRK-7845].

34. Mich. Dep't of State report, *supra* note 33, Audit Report at 1.

35. World Net Daily, *supra* note 33; *Oops! Stein's Recount Turns Up More Votes Than
Voters in Detroit*, Fox News Insider, Dec. 14, 2016, http://insider.foxnews.
com/2016/12/14/steins-recount-turns-more-votes-voters-detroit [https://perma.
cc/9LJY-7EK8]; @foxandfriends, Twitter, Dec. 14, 2016, 3:55 a.m. PST, https://
twitter.com/foxandfriends/status/809003930516496384 [https://perma.cc/AY6R-
6AZF]; John Wisely & JC Reindl, *Detroit's Election Woes: 782 More Votes Than Voters*,
Detroit Free Press, Dec. 18, 2016, http://www.freep.com/story/news/local/michigan/
detroit/2016/12/18/detroit-ballots-vote-recount-election-stein/95570866/ [https://
perma.cc/Q7SV-XX8Q].

36. Lawrence Norden, *Michigan Recount Exposes Voting Machine Failures*, Brennan
Ctr. for Just., Dec. 8, 2016, https://www.brennancenter.org/blog/michigan-recount-
exposes-voting-machine-failures [https://perma.cc/MRT3-EUEM]; Mich. Dep't of

State report, *supra* note 33, Audit Report at 2. The audit focused on the 136 precincts with the greatest anomalies, "the 'worst of the worst,' . . . including those having a significant number of misplaced ballots and those with unexplained mismatches in the number of voters compared to the number of ballots (plus or minus 3 or more)." *Id.*

37. Mich. Dep't of State report, *supra* note 33, Executive Summary at 2, Audit Report, at 2–3.

38. Mich. Dep't of State report, *supra* note 33, Executive Summary at 2.

39. A screenshot of the Georgia Secretary of State website from Nov. 4, 2018, is posted at @RickHasen, Twitter, Nov. 4. 2018, 12:54 p.m. PST, https://twitter.com/rickhasen/status/1059187255439372288 [https://perma.cc/HFJ7–5LFS]. Avi Selk, Vanessa Williams, & Amy Gardner, *Brian Kemp's Office Orders "Hacking" Probe of Georgia Democrats on Eve of Election He's Competing In*, Wash. Post, Nov. 4, 2018, https://www.washingtonpost.com/politics/2018/11/04/brian-kemps-office-orders-hacking-probe-georgia-democrats-eve-election-hes-competing/?utm_term=.68e3861af04e.

40. Jamil Smith, *Exclusive: In Leaked Audio, Brian Kemp Expresses Concern over Georgians Exercising Their Right to Vote*, Rolling Stone, Oct. 23, 2018, https://www.rollingstone.com/politics/politics-news/brian-kemp-leaked-audio-georgia-voting-745711/; Richard L. Hasen, *Brian Kemp Just Engaged in a Last-Minute Act of Banana-Republic Level Voter Manipulation in Georgia*, Slate, Nov. 4, 2018, https://slate.com/news-and-politics/2018/11/georgia-governor-candidate-brian-kemp-attempts-last-minute-banana-republic-style-voter-manipulation.html.

41. Kira Lerner, *The Powerful Role Confusion Plays in American Elections*, Talking Points Memo, Dec. 28, 2018, https://talkingpointsmemo.com/feature/the-powerful-role-confusion-plays-in-american-elections.

42. R. Robin McDonald, *Judge Denies Kemp's Effort to Postpone Absentee Voter TRO*, Nat'l L.J., Oct. 31, 2018, https://www.law.com/nationallawjournal/2018/10/31/judge-denies-kemps-effort-to-postpone-absentee-voter-tro/; Dartunorro Clark, *Judge Rules against Kemp over Voters Misidentified as Noncitizens*, NBC News, Nov. 2, 2018, https://www.nbcnews.com/politics/politics-news/judge-rules-against-kemp-over-voters-misidentified-noncitizens-n930536; Joshua Douglas, *Brian Kemp, If You Are Running in an Election, You Shouldn't Be Running the Election*, CNN Opinion, Nov. 5, 2018, https://www.cnn.com/2018/11/05/opinions/partisan-elections-futility-josh-douglas-opinion/index.html.

43. Johnny Kauffman, *Federal Court Asked to Scrap Georgia's 27,000 Electronic Voting Machines*, NPR, Sept. 12, 2018, https://www.npr.org/2018/09/12/646808300/

federal-court-asked-to-scrap-georgias-27–000-electronic-voting-machines; Alan Judd, *How Brian Kemp Turned Warning of Election System Vulnerability Against Democrats*, Atlanta Journal-Constitution, Dec. 14, 2018, https://www.ajc.com/news/state—regional-govt—politics/how-brian-kemp-turned-warning-election-system-vulnerability-against-democrats/iLOkpHK3ea39t8Eh4PCGxM/. The discussion of Georgia's cyber-vulnerabilities in this section draws from this detailed *Journal-Constitution* investigation.

44. Order, Curling. v. Kemp, No. 1:17-cv-2989-AT, at 5 (N.D. Ga., Sept. 17, 2018), https://assets.documentcloud.org/documents/4900825/Read-the-federal-judge-s-ruling-here.pdf [https://perma.cc/LM8Q-F9MC]. The judge later barred the use of DRE voting machinery without a paper trail after 2019. Order, Curling v. Raffensperger, No. 1:17-cv-2989 (N.D. Ga. Aug. 15, 2019), https://electionlawblog.org/wp-content/uploads/georgia-dre-decision.pdf [https://perma.cc/CS95-LZXW].

45. Jack Gillum, Jessica Huseman, Mike Tigas, Jeff Gao, & Stephen Fowler, *Georgia Officials Quietly Patched Security Holes They Said Didn't Exist*, ProPublica and Georgia Pub. Broadcasting, Nov. 5, 2018, https://www.propublica.org/article/georgia-officials-quietly-patched-security-holes-they-said-did-not-exist [https://perma.cc/FVL6-JG8L].

46. Richard L. Hasen, *Stacey Abrams' New Lawsuit against Georgia's Broken Voting System Is Incredibly Smart*, Slate, Nov. 27, 2018, https://slate.com/news-and-politics/2018/11/stacey-abrams-georgia-voting-rights-lawsuit.html.

Chapter 3. Dirty Tricks

1. Brian Lyman, *Russian Invasion? Roy Moore Sees Spike in Twitter Followers from the Land of Putin*, Montgomery Advertiser, Oct. 16, 2017, https://www.montgomery-advertiser.com/story/news/politics/southunionstreet/2017/10/16/roy-moores-twitter-account-gets-influx-russian-language-followers/768758001/.

2. Jessica Taylor, *Roy Moore, Culture Warrior, Will Be Favored to Be the Next U.S. Senator from Alabama*, NPR, Sept. 27, 2017, https://www.npr.org/2017/09/27/553856901/roy-moore-s-long-controversial-history-in-alabama-politics; Stephanie McCrummen, Beth Reinhard, & Alice Crites, *Woman Says Roy Moore Initiated Sexual Encounter When She Was 14, He Was 32*, Wash. Post, Nov. 9, 2017, https://www.washingtonpost.com/investigations/woman-says-roy-moore-initiated-sexual-encounter-when-she-was-14-he-was-32/2017/11/09/1f495878-c293–11e7-afe9–4f60b-5a6c4a0_story.html.

3. Lyman, *supra* note 1.

4. Although the *Washington Post* and *New York Times* reported on the leaked report, they have not released it. Scott Shane & Alan Blinder, *Secret Experiment in Alabama Senate Race Imitated Russian Tactics*, N.Y. Times, Dec. 19, 2018, https://www.nytimes.com/2018/12/19/us/alabama-senate-roy-jones-russia.html; Scott Shane, Alan Blinder, & Sydney Ember, *Doug Jones "Outraged" by Russian-Style Tactics Used in His Senate Race*, N.Y. Times, Dec. 20, 2018, https://www.nytimes.com/2018/12/20/us/politics/doug-jones-social-media.html; Craig Timberg, Tony Romm, Aaron C. Davis, & Elizabeth Dwoskin, *Secret Campaign to Use Russian-Inspired Tactics in 2017 Ala. Election Stirs Anxiety for Democrats*, Wash. Post, Jan. 6, 2019, https://www.washingtonpost.com/business/technology/secret-campaign-to-use-russian-inspired-tactics-in-2017-alabama-election-stirs-anxiety-for-democrats/2019/01/06/58803f26–0400–11e9–8186–4ec26a485713_story.html. A Medium page by Jeff Giesea contains what appear to be six pages of the twelve-page report. Jeff Giesea, *BREAKING: Here's The After-Action Report from the Alabama Senate Disinformation Campaign*, Medium, Dec. 27, 2018, https://medium.com/@jeffgiesea/breaking-heres-the-after-action-report-from-the-alabama-senate-disinformation-campaign-e3edd854f17d [https://perma.cc/LJX7-ZGLT].

5. Scott Shane & Alan Blinder, *Democrats Faked Online Push to Outlaw Alcohol in Alabama Race*, N.Y. Times, Jan. 7, 2019, https://www.nytimes.com/2019/01/07/us/politics/alabama-senate-facebook-roy-moore.html.

6. Timberg, Romm, Davis, & Dwoskin, *supra* note 4.

7. Dmitri Mehlhorn, *Investing in US, 2017–2018 in Review*, Medium, Dec. 21, 2018, https://medium.com/@DmitriMehlhorn/investing-in-us-64afe222face [https://perma.cc/EE5N-S4ZT]; Scott Shane, *LinkedIn Co-Founder Apologizes for Deception in Alabama Senate Race*, N.Y. Times, Dec. 26, 2018, https://www.nytimes.com/2018/12/26/us/reid-hoffman-alabama-election-disinformation.html.

8. Scott Shane, *Facebook Closes 5 Accounts Tied to Russia-Like Tactics in Alabama Senate Race*, N.Y. Times, Dec. 22, 2018, https://www.nytimes.com/2018/12/22/us/politics/facebook-suspends-alabama-elections.html; Tony Romm & Craig Timberg, *Facebook Suspends Five Accounts, Including That of a Social Media Researcher, for Misleading Tactics in Alabama Election*, Wash. Post, Dec. 22, 2018, https://www.washingtonpost.com/technology/2018/12/22/facebook-suspends-five-accounts-including-social-media-researcher-misleading-tactics-alabama-election/; Shane, *supra* note 7; New Knowledge, *New Knowledge Research in Alabama*, Dec. 28, 2018, https://www.newknowledge.com/articles/new-knowledge-research-in-alabama/ [https://perma.cc/DCP2-BXPG].

9. Joohn Choe, *The Resistance Information Warfare Handbook, Part IV*, Medium, Apr. 2, 2018, https://medium.com/@joohnchoe/the-resistance-information-warfare-handbook-part-iv-a375993f3dc0 [https://perma.cc/XP5V-PW2M]; Jonathon Morgan, *Social Media and the Alabama Special Election*, Medium, Jan. 2, 2019, https://medium.com/@jonathonmorgan/social-media-and-the-alabama-special-election-c83350324529 [https://perma.cc/737A-PPAG]; Matt Osborne, *Roy Moore and the Politics of Alcohol in Alabama*, LinkedIn, Aug. 9, 2018, https://www.linkedin.com/pulse/roy-moore-politics-alcohol-alabama-matt-osborne/ [https://perma.cc/YEB4-3JN2]; Tovo Labs, *Proof of Digital Persuasion in Alabama's Senate Race*, Medium, Apr. 7, 2018, https://medium.com/@david.goldstein_4168/https-medium-com-tovolabs-proof-of-digital-persuasion-in-alabama-senate-race-85a517481371 [https://perma.cc/EXE7-3CF5].

10. Glenn Stephens, *Almost $50 Million Spent in Alabama's U.S. Special Senate Election*, Birmingham Watch, Jan. 30, 2018, https://birminghamwatch.org/almost-50-million-spent-jones-moore-u-s-senate-election/; Alan Blinder, *Alabama Certifies Jones Win, Brushing Aside Challenge from Roy Moore*, N.Y. Times, Dec. 28, 2017, https://www.nytimes.com/2017/12/28/us/politics/roy-moore-block-election.html.

11. Jessica Taylor, *Fact Check: Where Roy Moore's Voter Fraud Claims Fall Flat*, NPR, Dec. 28, 2017, https://www.npr.org/2017/12/28/574222257/fact-check-where-roy-moores-voter-fraud-claims-fall-flat; Craig Timberg & Tony Romm, *Disinformation Campaign Targeting Roy Moore's Senate Bid May Have Violated Law, Alabama Attorney General Says*, Wash. Post, Dec. 27, 2018, https://www.washingtonpost.com/technology/2018/12/27/disinformation-campaign-targeting-roy-moores-senate-bid-may-have-violated-law-alabama-attorney-general-says/?utm_term=.22311971829f; Shane, Blinder, & Ember, *supra* note 4.

12. New Knowledge, *The Tactics and Tropes of the Internet Research Agency*, at 4, Dec. 17, 2018, https://cdn2.hubspot.net/hubfs/4326998/ira-report-rebrand_FinalJ14.pdf [https://perma.cc/9FGQ-TMGM]. Much of this ground is covered in volume 1 of the report of Robert Mueller, the special counsel appointed to investigate Russian interference in the 2016 presidential election. See Special Counsel Robert S. Mueller III, *Report on the Investigation into Russian Interference in the 2016 Presidential Election* (Mar. 2019). The official version appears at https://www.justice.gov/storage/report.pdf, and a searchable version appears at https://www.documentcloud.org/documents/5955379-Redacted-Mueller-Report.html#document/ [https://perma.cc/9TEW-JD3Z].

13. *New Knowledge*, *supra* note 12, at 7–8; Philip N. Howard et al., *The IRA, Social Media and Political Polarization in the United States, 2012–2018*, Working Paper

2018.2, Oxford, UK: Project on Computational Propaganda, https://comprop.oii.
ox.ac.uk/research/ira-political-polarization/ [https://perma.cc/GW3J-L5A6]; Ryan
Lucas, *How Russia Used Facebook to Organize Two Sets of Protesters*, NPR, Nov. 1,
2017, https://www.npr.org/2017/11/01/561427876/how-russia-used-facebook-to-
organize-two-sets-of-protesters.

14. *Mueller, supra* note 12, at vol. 1, p. 29.

15. On the $6.5 billion figure, see Christopher Ingraham, *Somebody Just Put a
Price Tag on the 2016 Election. It's a Doozy*, Wash. Post, Apr. 14, 2017, https://www.
washingtonpost.com/news/wonk/wp/2017/04/14/somebody-just-put-a-price-tag-
on-the-2016-election-its-a-doozy/.

16. *Mueller, supra* note 12, at vol. 1, pp. 1–2.

17. Adam Entous & Ronan Farrow, *Private Mossad for Hire: Inside an Effort to Influence American Elections, Starting with One Small-Town Race*, New Yorker, Feb. 18 & 25,
2019, https://www.newyorker.com/magazine/2019/02/18/private-mossad-for-hire ("according to the Nader representative, shortly after the election Zamel bragged to Nader
that he had conducted a secret campaign that had been influential in Trump's victory.
Zamel agreed to brief Nader on how the operation had worked. During that conversation, Zamel showed Nader several analytical reports, including one that described the
role of avatars, bots, fake news, and unattributed Web sites in assisting Trump. Zamel
told Nader, 'Here's the work that we did to help get Trump elected,' according to the
Nader representative. Nader paid Zamel more than two million dollars, but never
received copies of the reports, that person said."); Scott Shane & Vindu Goel, *Fake
Russian Facebook Accounts Bought $100,000 in Political Ads*, N.Y. Times, Sept. 6, 2017,
https://nyti.ms/2xPJom9; see also Scott Shane, *The Fake Americans Russia Created to
Influence the Election*, N.Y. Times, Sept. 7, 2017, https://nyti.ms/2xdVuXM (describing
fake profiles of Americans backed by Russians tweeting campaign messages); Marshall
Cohen, *By the Numbers: The Trump Orbit's Contact with Russians*, CNN, Nov. 22, 2017,
http://www.cnn.com/2017/11/21/politics/trump-russia-by-the-numbers/index.html
("At least 12 Trump associates had contacts with Russians during the campaign or
transition."); Mark Mazzetti, Ronen Bergman, David D. Kirkpatrick, & Maggie
Haberman, *Rick Gates Sought Online Manipulation Plans from Israeli Intelligence Firm
for Trump Campaign*, N.Y. Times, Oct. 8, 2018, https://www.nytimes.com/2018/10/08/
us/politics/rick-gates-psy-group-trump.html; Mark Mazzetti, Ronen Bergman, &
David D. Kirkpatrick, *Trump Jr. and Other Aides Met with Gulf Emissary Offering Help
to Win Election*, N.Y. Times, May 19, 2018, https://www.nytimes.com/2018/05/19/us/
politics/trump-jr-saudi-uae-nader-prince-zamel.html; Josh Gerstein, *Mueller Witness*

Was Convicted on Child Porn Charge, Politico, Mar. 16, 2018, https://www.politico. com/story/2018/03/16/george-nader-child-porn-467776. Federal officials later indicted Nader on new child pornography charges based upon information that came to light from cell phones seized as part of Mueller's investigation. Mark Mazzetti, *Witness in Mueller Inquiry Is Arrested on Child Pornography Charges*, N.Y. Times, June 3, 2019, https://www.nytimes.com/2019/06/03/us/politics/george-nader-child-pornography-arrest.html.

The next few paragraphs draw from Richard L. Hasen, *The 2016 U.S. Voting Wars: From Bad to Worse*, 26 Wm. & Mary Bill of Rts. J. 629 (2018).

18. Office of the Dir. of Nat'l Intelligence, ICA 2017-01D, Assessing Russian Activities and Intentions in Recent US Elections, at ii (2017), https://www.dni.gov/files/documents/ICA_2017_01.pdf [https://perma.cc/96H7–2K8Z] (emphases omitted). The "key judgments" also included the following: "We also assess Putin and the Russian Government aspired to help President-elect Trump's election chances when possible by discrediting Secretary Clinton and publicly contrasting her unfavorably to him. All three agencies agree with this judgment. CIA and FBI have high confidence in this judgment; NSA has moderate confidence" (emphases omitted); see also Greg Miller et al., *Obama's Secret Struggle to Punish Russia for Putin's Election Assault*, Wash. Post, June 23, 2017, https://www.washingtonpost.com/graphics/2017/world/national-security/obama-putin-election-hacking/?utm_term=.6e02e087764a ("[American] intelligence captured Putin's specific instructions on the operation's audacious objectives—defeat or at least damage the Democratic nominee, Hillary Clinton, and help elect her opponent, Donald Trump.").

19. See Office of the Dir. of Nat'l Intelligence, *supra* note 18, at 3 ("Russia's state-run propaganda machine—comprised of its domestic media apparatus, outlets targeting global audiences such as RT and Sputnik, and a network of quasi-government trolls—contributed to the influence campaign by serving as a platform for Kremlin messaging to Russian and international audiences. State-owned Russian media made increasingly favorable comments about President-elect Trump as the 2016 US general and primary election campaigns progressed while consistently offering negative coverage of Secretary Clinton."); *id.* at Annex A, at 6 (describing Russian propaganda activities aimed at the United States). For example, RT America "portrayed the US electoral process as undemocratic and featured calls by US protesters for the public to rise up and 'take this government back.'" *Id.* See also Lauren Carroll, *Russia and Its Influence on the Presidential Election*, PolitiFact, Dec. 1, 2016, http://www.politifact.com/truth-o-meter/article/2016/dec/01/russia-and-its-influence-presidential-election/

[https://perma.cc/6UFD-QKUF]; Louis Jacobson, *Donald Trump Incorrectly Pins Benghazi Criticism on Sidney Blumenthal*, PolitiFact, Oct. 11, 2016, 2:34 p.m., http://www.politifact.com/truth-o-meter/statements/2016/oct/11/donald-trump/donald-trump-incorrectly-pins-benghazi-criticism-s/ [https://perma.cc/5ZWJ-XGDP]; Shane & Goel, *supra* note 17; Massimo Calabresi, *Inside Russia's Social Media War on America*, Time, May 18, 2017, http://time.com/4783932/inside-russia-social-media-war-america/ ("Congressional investigators are looking at how Russia helped stories like these spread to specific audiences. Counterintelligence officials, meanwhile, have picked up evidence that Russia tried to target particular influencers during the election season who they reasoned would help spread the damaging stories. These officials have seen evidence of Russia using its algorithmic techniques to target the social media accounts of particular reporters, senior intelligence officials tell Time. 'It's not necessarily the journal or the newspaper or the TV show,' says the senior intelligence official. 'It's the specific reporter that they find who might be a little bit slanted toward believing things, and they'll hit him' with a flood of fake news stories. Russia plays in every social media space. The intelligence officials have found that Moscow's agents bought ads on Facebook to target specific populations with propaganda. 'They buy the ads, where it says sponsored by—they do that just as much as anybody else does,' says the senior intelligence official. (A Facebook official says the company has no evidence of that occurring.) The ranking Democrat on the Senate Intelligence Committee, Mark Warner of Virginia, has said he is looking into why, for example, four of the top five Google search results the day the U.S. released a report on the 2016 operation were links to Russia's TV propaganda arm, RT. (Google says it saw no meddling in this case.) Researchers at the University of Southern California, meanwhile, found that nearly 20% of political tweets in 2016 between Sept. 16 and Oct. 21 were generated by bots of unknown origin; investigators are trying to figure out how many were Russian.").

20. New Knowledge, *supra* note 12, at 8, 11, 13, 16, 45–46; Howard et al., *supra* note 13, at 9–10.

21. *Id.* at 34; Richard Engel, Kate Benyon-Tinker, & Kennett Werner, *Russian Documents Reveal Desire to Sow Racial Discord—and Violence—in the U.S.*, NBC News, May 20, 2019, https://www.nbcnews.com/news/world/russian-documents-reveal-desire-sow-racial-discord-violence-u-s-n1008051.

22. Howard et al., *supra* note 13, at 76–77. On the most shared Hillary Clinton post being the one about illegal voting, see p. 51 of the slide deck accompanying the New Knowledge report, posted at https://cdn2.hubspot.net/hubfs/4326998/

SSCI%20Presentation%20final.pdf [https://perma.cc/N8L4-S7AF]. Damian Dovarganes, AP Images, *California Hispanics*, Aug. 15, 2012, http://www.apimages. com/metadata/Index/California-Hispanics/41af1e6fdfec4e45adcc2efdcbe6e571/36/0 [https://perma.cc/V9CX-JD2U].

23. The indictment, filed Feb. 16, 2018, is posted at https://www.justice.gov/ file/1035477/download [https://perma.cc/3T8R-U2U3]. The Kavanaugh case is Bluman v. FEC, 800 F. Supp. 2d 281, 292, *aff'd*, 565 U.S. 1104 (2012). For an analysis of the constitutional and statutory questions surrounding whether the Russian advertisements were illegal, see Richard L. Hasen, *Cheap Speech and What It Has Done (to American Democracy)*, 16 First Amend. L. Rev. 200, 218–21 (2018).

24. *Id.* at 221–26; Richard L. Hasen, *A Constitutional Right to Lie in Campaigns and Elections?* 74 Mont. L. Rev. 53 (2013); Roger Parloff, *Exclusive: Facebook Ex-Security Chief: How "Hypertargeting" Threatens Democracy*, Yahoo! Finance, Feb. 8, 2019, https://finance.yahoo.com/news/facebook-security-officer-alex-stamos-targeting-risk-142859539.html.

25. Nathaniel Persily, *The Internet's Challenge to Democracy: Framing the Problem and Assessing Reform* 22–23 (2019), https://storage.googleapis.com/kofiannanfoundation.org/2019/02/a6112278–190206_kaf_democracy_internet_persily_single_pages_v3.pdf [https://perma.cc/A97Z-72PX].

26. Brendan Nyhan, *Why Fears of Fake News Are Overhyped*, Medium, Feb. 4, 2018, https://medium.com/s/reasonable-doubt/why-fears-of-fake-news-are-overhyped-2ed9ca0a52c9 [https://perma.cc/V877-RKCD]; Bobby Chesney & Danielle Citron, *Deep Fakes: A Looming Challenge for Privacy, Democracy, and National Security* (draft at 5), 107 Calif. L. Rev. (forthcoming 2019), *draft available at* https://papers. ssrn.com/sol3/papers.cfm?abstract_id=3213954; Samantha Cole, *We Are Truly Fucked: Everyone Is Making AI-Generated Fake Porn Now*, Motherboard, Jan. 24, 2018, https:// motherboard.vice.com/en_us/article/bjye8a/reddit-fake-porn-app-daisy-ridley [https://perma.cc/RN69-U97V].

27. Professor Levitt made the remarks at a forum entitled Voting Rights and Wrongs held at the UCLA Hammer Museum on Jan. 31, 2019. The remark appears at the 31:23 mark on the video of the event, posted at https://livestream.com/ accounts/5045103/events/8520207/videos/186666756 [https://perma.cc/R3KW-66FD]. See also Justin Levitt, *Kavanaugh, Foreign Agents, and American Elections*, Take Care Blog, Sept. 5, 2018, https://takecareblog.com/blog/kavanaugh-foreign-agents-and-american-elections [https://perma.cc/X39R-4ZG2].

28. Much of this story is covered in vol. 1 of Mueller, *supra* note 12. The next two paragraphs draw from Hasen, *supra* note 17, at 644–46.

29. Sam Frizell, *What Leaked Emails Reveal about Hillary Clinton's Campaign*, Time, Oct. 7, 2016, http://time.com/4523749/hillary-clinton-wikileaks-leaked-emails-john-podesta/; Jonathan Martin & Alan Rappeport, *Debbie Wasserman Schultz to Resign D.N.C. Post*, N.Y. Times, July 24, 2016, https://nyti.ms/2kTxyT7; Michael Sainato, Opinion, *DC Leaks Exposes Clinton Insider's Elitist and Embarrassing Emails*, Observer, Oct. 7, 2016, http://www.observer.com/2016/10/dc-leaks-exposes-clinton-insiders-elitist-and-embarrassing-emails [https://perma.cc/XU3V-P5UN]; Cory Bennett, *Guccifer 2.0 Drops More DNC Docs*, Politico, Sept. 13, 2016, https://www.politico.com/story/2016/09/guccifer-2-0-dnc-docs-228091; Matthew Rosenberg & Maggie Haberman, *Trump Adviser Had Twitter Contact with Figure Tied to Russians*, N.Y. Times, Mar. 11, 2017, https://nyti.ms/2mdQtFx. In addition, Donald Trump Jr. exchanged direct messages over Twitter with WikiLeaks. See Julia Ioffe, *The Secret Correspondence between Donald Trump Jr. and WikiLeaks*, Atlantic, Nov. 13, 2017, https://www.theatlantic.com/politics/archive/2017/11/the-secret-correspondence-between-donald-trump-jr-and-wikileaks/545738/; Devlin Barrett, Rosalind S. Helderman, Lori Rozsa, & Manuel Roig-Franzia, *Longtime Trump Advisor Roger Stone Indicted by Special Counsel in Russia Investigation*, Wash. Post, Jan. 25, 2019, https://www.washingtonpost.com/politics/longtime-trump-adviser-roger-stone-indicted-by-special-counsel-in-russia-investigation/2019/01/25/93a4d8fa-2093-11e9-8e21-59a09ffie2a1_story.html.

30. @alexstamos, Twitter, Nov. 15, 2018, 11:35 a.m. PST, https://twitter.com/alexstamos/status/1063153495770046464 [https://perma.cc/TL3J-SXVQ]; Parloff, *supra* note 24.

31. *Mueller, supra* note 12, at vol. 1, p. 50; Ellen Nakashima & Karoun Demirjian, *Russian Government Hackers Targeted Small County in Florida Panhandle in 2016*, Wash. Post, May 16, 2019, https://www.washingtonpost.com/world/national-security/floridas-house-members-demand-changes-to-disclosure-rules-on-election-hacking/2019/05/16/8e039672-77f8-11e9-bd25-c989555e7766_story.html.

32. Michael Riley & Jordan Robertson, *Russian Cyber Hacks on U.S. Voting System Far Wider Than Previously Known*, Bloomberg, June 13, 2017, https://www.bloomberg.com/news/articles/2017-06-13/russian-breach-of-39-states-threatens-future-u-s-elections [https://perma.cc/ME58-TREC]. A DHS official testified in June 2017 that hackers targeted twenty-one state election systems. See Dustin Volz &

Julia Edwards Ainsley, *Russians Targeted 21 Election Systems, U.S. Official Says*, Reuters June 21, 2017, http://www.reuters.com/article/us-usa-cyber-congress-idUSKBN19 C1Y3?utm_campaign [https:// perma.cc/A3WB-SVSX]; Massimo Calabresi, *Election Hackers Altered Voter Rolls, Stole Private Data, Officials Say*, Time, June 22, 2017, http://time.com/4828306/russian-hacking-election-widespread-private-data/; Hearing Before the H. Permanent Select Comm. on Intelligence, 115th Cong. 2–6 (2017) (statement of Jeh Charles Johnson, former secretary of Homeland Security); Frances Robles, *Russian Hackers Were "in a Position" to Alter Florida Voting Rolls, Rubio Confirms*, N.Y. Times, Aug. 26, 2019, https://www.nytimes.com/2019/04/26/us/florida-russia-hacking-election.html.

33. Mark Niesse, *Georgia Voters Suing for Paper Ballots Win Appeal to 11th Circuit*, Atlanta Journal-Const., Feb. 8, 2019, https://www.ajc.com/news/state—regional-govt—politics/georgia-voters-suing-for-paper-ballots-win-appeal-11th-circuit/1HWhP8xNyo81ONfesFxLOM/. On Kemp's refusal to accept DHS help, see chapter 2.

34. Chesney & Citron, *supra* note 26 (draft at 22).

35. Rebecca Smith & Rob Barry, *America's Electric Grid Has a Vulnerable Back Door—and Russia Walked through It*, Wall St. J., Jan. 10, 2019, https://www.wsj.com/articles/americas-electric-grid-has-a-vulnerable-back-doorand-russia-walked-through-it-11547137112.

36. *Id.*

37. Andy Greenberg, *How an Entire Nation Became Russia's Test Lab for Cyberwar*, Wired, June 20, 2017, https://www.wired.com/story/russian-hackers-attack-ukraine/.

38. *Id.*; see also Donghui Park, Julia Summers, & Michael Walstrom, *Cyberattack on Critical Infrastructure: Russian and the Ukrainian Power Grid Attacks*, University of Washington, Henry M. Jackson School of International Studies, Oct. 11, 2017, https://jsis.washington.edu/news/cyberattack-critical-infrastructure-russia-ukrainian-power-grid-attacks/ [https://perma.cc/4D99-EWXE].

39. Michael T. Morley, *Election Emergencies: Voting in the Wake of Natural Disasters and Terrorist Attacks*, 67 Emory L.J. 545 (2018); Eric A. Fischer et al., Cong. Research Serv., RL 32654, Safeguarding Federal Elections from Possible Terrorist Attack: Issues and Options for Congress (2004) [https://perma.cc/B4TP-6P3G]; John C. Fortier & Norman J. Ornstein, *If Terrorists Attacked Our Presidential Election*, 3 Election L.J. 597 (2004); Jerry H. Goldfeder, *Could Terrorists Derail a Presidential Election?* 32 Fordham Urb. L.J. 523 (2005); Steven H. Huefner, *Withstanding Election Day Terrorism*, Election L. @ Moritz (July 19, 2004), http://moritzlaw.osu.edu/electionlaw/ebook/part7/elections_preso2.html [https://perma.cc/3NSP-KYFR].

40. Norman J. Ornstein, *Our Elections Are Wide-Open for a Constitutional Crisis*, Wash. Post, Oct. 26, 2018, https://www.washingtonpost.com/opinions/our-elections-are-wide-open-for-a-constitutional-crisis/2018/10/26/317cb7e0-d86a-11e8–83a2-d1c3da28d6b6_story.html/.

41. Ballotpedia, North Carolina's 9th Congressional District Election, 2016, https://ballotpedia.org/North_Carolina%27s_9th_Congressional_District_election,_2016 [https://perma.cc/VSU8-TXVL]; U.S. Census Bureau, Quick Facts: Bladen County, North Carolina, https://www.census.gov/quickfacts/bladencountynorthcarolina [https://perma.cc/XQ5G-RZGS]; Emery P. Dalesio, *Mark Harris Says Background Check on McCrae Dowless Missed His Felonies*, AP, Feb. 11, 2019, https://talkingpointsmemo.com/news/mark-harris-background-check-mccrae-dowless-undecided-north-carolina-house-race [https://perma.cc/5EKV-FA4D].

42. *Id.*

43. Leigh Ann Caldwell, Rich Gardella, & Ben Kamisar, *In N.C. Election Fraud Case, Witness Says Operative Held onto 800 Absentee Ballots*, NBC News, Dec. 11, 2018, https://www.nbcnews.com/politics/politics-news/n-c-election-fraud-case-witness-says-operative-held-800-n946831; Richard Fausset, Alan Blinder, Sydney Ember, Timothy Williams, & Serge F. Kovaleski, *North Carolina's "Guru of Elections": Can-Do Operator Who May Have Done Too Much*, N.Y. Times, Dec. 8, 2018, https://www.nytimes.com/2018/12/08/us/politics/north-carolina-election-fraud-dowless.html.

44. *Id.*; Brianna Sacks & Otillia Steadman, *Inside the North Carolina Republican Vote Machine: Cash, Pills—And Ballots*, Buzzfeed News, Dec. 5, 2018, https://www.buzzfeednews.com/article/briannasacks/dowless-britt-inside-north-carolina-absentee-ballot-machine [https://perma.cc/NGD9–8RUN].

45. Beth Reinhard, *Justice Officials Were Briefed Months Ago on Allegations against Operative at Center of N.C. Election Fraud Scandal*, Wash. Post, Jan. 11, 2019, https://www.washingtonpost.com/investigations/justice-officials-from-washington-were-briefed-months-ago-on-allegations-against-mccrae-dowless-operative-at-center-of-nc-election-fraud-scandal/2019/01/11/4c333722–15db-11e9-a896-f104373c7ffd_story.html.

46. Travis Fain & Laura Leslie, *DOJ Delays Subpoenas on Voting Data until "Well After" Election*, WRAL, Sept. 7, 2018, https://www.wral.com/doj-delays-subpoenas-on-voting-data-until-well-after-election/17824074/; Amy Gardner, Beth Reinhard, & Alice Crites, *Trump-Appointed Prosecutor Focused on Allegations of Voter Fraud by Immigrants amid Warnings about Separate Ballot Scheme*, Wash. Post, Feb. 3, 2019, https://www.washingtonpost.com/politics/trump-appointed-prosecutor-focused-

on-allegations-of-voting-fraud-by-immigrants-amid-warnings-about-separate-ballot-scheme/2019/02/03/989851c2–19de-11e9–8813-cb9dec761e73_story.html.

47. *Id.*

48. Sam Levine, *She Helped Her Boyfriend Register to Vote. Now She's Going to Prison for It*, HuffPost, Feb. 8, 2019, https://www.huffingtonpost.com/entry/north-carolina-non-citizen-voting_us_5c5dd26fe4b0eec79b2336ff; Eli Rosenberg, *A Grandma Helped Her Boyfriend Register to Vote. She Was Just Sentenced to Prison for It*, Wash. Post, Feb. 9, 2019, https://www.washingtonpost.com/politics/2019/02/09/grandma-helped-her-boyfriend-register-vote-she-was-just-sentenced-prison-it/. *HuffPost* posted the transcript of the sentencing hearing for Paige at https://assets.documentcloud.org/documents/5732518/Denslo-Allen-Paige-Sentencing-Hearing.pdf [https://perma.cc/8BPS-6LMY].

49. U.S. Attorney's Office, Eastern District of North Carolina, press release, *Former North Carolina Board of Elections Election Official Sentenced to Prison for Aiding and Abetting Voting by an Alien in the 2016 General Election*, Feb. 8, 2019, https://www.justice.gov/usao-ednc/pr/former-north-carolina-board-elections-election-official-sentenced-prison-aiding-and [https://perma.cc/8UM6-YKY5].

50. Amy Gardner & John Wagner, *N.C. Political Operative Indicted, and Prosecutor Signals That More Charges Are Likely*, Wash. Post, Feb. 28, 2019, https://www.washingtonpost.com/politics/north-carolina-political-operative-indicted-in-election-fraud-case-that-upended-congressional-race/2019/02/27/b0d5f004–3aaf-11e9-aaae-69364b2ed137_story.html; Amy Gardner, *Federal Grand Jury Issues Subpoenas in N.C. Election Fraud Investigation*, Wash. Post, Mar. 12, 2019, https://www.washingtonpost.com/politics/federal-grand-jury-issues-subpoenas-in-nc-election-fraud-investigation/2019/03/12/3ee7010e-44e6–11e9-aaf8–4512a6fe3439_story.html.

51. Eric Schmitt, David E. Sanger, & Maggie Haberman, *In Push for 2020 Election Security, Top Official Was Warned: Don't Tell Trump*, N.Y. Times, Apr. 24, 2019, https://www.nytimes.com/2019/04/24/us/politics/russia-2020-election-trump.html.

Chapter 4. "Stolen"

1. *Donald Trump Campaign Rally in Ambridge, Pennsylvania*, C-SPAN, Oct. 10, 2016 (video), https://www.c-span.org/video/?416683–1/donald-trump-campaigns-ambridge-pennsylvania&start=2788. The quoted remarks appear at the forty-six-minute mark on the video.

2. Ashley Parker, *Donald Trump, Slipping in Polls, Warns of "Stolen" Election*, N.Y. Times, Oct. 13, 2016, https://www.nytimes.com/2016/10/14/us/politics/trump-election-rigging.html.

3. Philip Bump, *Donald Trump Warns That "Other Communities" Are Poised to Steal the Election*, Wash. Post, Oct. 11, 2016, https://www.washingtonpost.com/news/the-fix/wp/2016/10/11/donald-trump-warns-that-other-communities-are-poised-to-steal-the-election/?utm_term=.f1019e31aff0; Melanie Mizenko, *Crowd Roars at Donald Trump's Second Appearance in Wilkes-Barre Township*, Times Leader, Oct. 10, 2016, https://www.timesleader.com/news/local/595662/crowd-roars-at-donald-trumps-second-appearance-in-wilkes-barre-townshippage/12/.

4. Robert Farley, *Fact Check: Trump's Bogus Voter Fraud Claims*, USA Today, Oct. 19, 2016, https://www.usatoday.com/story/news/politics/elections/2016/10/19/fact-check-trump-bogus-voter-fraud-claims/92434104/; Jenna Johnson, *Donald Trump Says the Election Is "Rigged." Here's What His Supporters Think That Means*, Wash. Post, Oct. 18, 2016, https://www.washingtonpost.com/news/post-politics/wp/2016/10/18/donald-trump-says-the-election-is-rigged-heres-what-his-supporters-think-that-means/?utm_term=.7d4caf2a7157; @realdonaldtrump, Twitter, Oct. 16, 2016, 10:01 a.m. PST, https://twitter.com/realDonaldTrump/status/787699930718695425 [https://perma.cc/MZ6R-6WA7].

5. @realdonaldtrump, Twitter, Oct. 17, 2016, 5:33 a.m. PST, https://twitter.com/realDonaldTrump/status/787995025527410688 [https://perma.cc/MMY2-RJMQ]; Mahita Gajanan, *Donald Trump Claims Election Will Be Rigged at Polling Sites*, Time, Oct. 17, 2016, http://time.com/4532679/donald-trump-election-rigged/.

6. Democratic Nat'l Comm. v. Republican Nat'l Comm., 2016 WL 6584915, *6 (D.N.J. Nov. 5, 2016).

7. Jenna Johnson, *Donald Trump to African American and Hispanic Voters: "What Do You Have to Lose?"* Wash. Post, Aug. 22, 2016, https://www.washingtonpost.com/news/post-politics/wp/2016/08/22/donald-trump-to-african-american-and-hispanic-voters-what-do-you-have-to-lose/.

8. *Democratic Nat'l Comm.*, 2016 WL 6584915 at *17.

9. The video appears at https://www.youtube.com/watch?v=KQJzt48wXbA (last visited May 21, 2019).

10. Jeremy Diamond, *Donald Trump, "I Will Totally Accept" Election Results "If I Win,"* CNN, Oct. 20, 2016, https://www.cnn.com/2016/10/20/politics/donald-trump-i-will-totally-accept-election-results-if-i-win/index.html.

11. Kirby Goidel, Keith Gaddie, & Spencer Goidel, *Rigged-Election Rhetoric: Coverage and Consequences*, 52 P.S.: Pol. Sci. & Pol. 229 (2019), https://www.cambridge.org/core/journals/ps-political-science-and-politics/article/riggedelection-rhetoric-coverage-and-consequences/A3BE9663C193A313C7BFC5AD6FBCAC7E.

12. Adriano Udani & David Kimball, *Immigrant Resentment and Voter Fraud Beliefs in the U.S. Electorate*, 46 Am. Pol. Res. 402 (2018).

13. Anthony Man, *Trump Bashes Broward County and Brenda Snipes over Election Issues*, S. Fla. Sun-Sentinel, Nov. 9, 2018, https://www.sun-sentinel.com/news/politics/fl-ne-florida-voting-ballots-senate-friday-20181109-story.html.

14. Alex Daugherty, *Trump, Scott and Rubio Continue to Push Claims of Florida Voter Fraud without Evidence*, Miami Herald, Nov. 12, 2018, https://www.miamiherald.com/news/politics-government/article221528685.html; Colby Itkowitz, *Paul Ryan Isn't Saying There Was Voter Fraud in California. But . . .*, Wash. Post, Nov. 29, 2018, https://www.washingtonpost.com/politics/2018/11/29/paul-ryan-isnt-saying-there-was-voter-fraud-california/.

15. Monika Bauerlein & Clara Jeffery, *How Facebook Screwed Us All*, Mother Jones, Mar./Apr. 2019, https://www.motherjones.com/politics/2019/02/how-facebook-screwed-us-all/.

16. Democratic Nat'l Comm. v. Republican Nat'l Comm., 2016 WL 6584915, *2 (D.N.J. 2016) (citations omitted). The additional facts in the next few paragraphs are drawn from this court opinion.

17. Democratic Nat'l Comm., v. Republican Nat'l Comm., 671 F. Supp. 2d 575, (D.N.J. 2009), *aff'd*, 673 F.3d 192 (3d Cir. 2012), *cert. denied*, 568 U.S. 1138 (2013).

18. This paragraph and the next few paragraphs draw from Richard L. Hasen, *Vote Suppressors Unleashed*, Slate, Nov. 27, 2017, https://slate.com/news-and-politics/2017/11/donald-trump-will-supercharge-voter-suppression-if-the-rnc-consent-decree-falls.html; and Richard L. Hasen, *Donald Trump Was Just Handed a Chance to Supercharge Voter Suppression in 2020*, Slate, Jan. 8, 2019, https://slate.com/news-and-politics/2019/01/donald-trump-voter-suppression-plan-2020.html. The original *Politico* article mentioning Spicer's role is Anni Karni & Josh Gerstein, *Spicer's Election-Night Memories Cause Anxiety in the GOP*, Politico, Nov. 10, 2017, https://www.politico.com/story/2017/11/10/sean-spicer-gq-magazine-story-fallout-244784. The *GQ* report is Ben Schreckinger, *Inside Donald Trump's Election Night War Room*, GQ, Nov. 7, 2017, https://www.gq.com/story/inside-donald-trumps-election-night-war-room.

19. Democratic Nat'l Comm. v. Republican Nat'l Comm., 2019 WL 117555, *1 & n.5 (3d Cir. Jan. 7, 2019).

20. Gabriel Debenedetti, *Trump Takes Control of the GOP Machine*, Politico, Apr. 11, 2017, https://www.politico.com/story/2017/04/trump-republican-party-takeover-states-237075.

21. Richard L. Hasen, *Brian Kemp Just Engaged in a Last-Minute Act of Banana-Republic Level Voter Manipulation in Georgia*, Slate, Nov. 4, 2018, https://slate.com/news-and-politics/2018/11/georgia-governor-candidate-brian-kemp-attempts-last-minute-banana-republic-style-voter-manipulation.html.

22. Peter Esaiasson, *Electoral Losers Revisited—How Citizens React to Defeat at the Ballot Box*, 30 Electoral Stud. 102, 112 (2011); Richard Nadeau & André Blais, *Accepting the Election Outcome: The Effect of Participation on Losers' Consent*, 23 Brit. J. Pol. Sci. 553 (2009).

23. David Marchese, *Talk: Why Stacey Abrams Is Still Saying She Won*, N.Y. Times Mag., Apr. 28, 2019, https://www.nytimes.com/interactive/2019/04/28/magazine/stacey-abrams-election-georgia.html; Ian Schwartz, *Sen. Sherrod Brown: If Stacey Abrams Doesn't Win in Georgia, Republicans "Stole" It*, RealClearPolitics, Nov. 14, 2018, https://www.realclearpolitics.com/video/2018/11/14/sen_sherrod_brown_if_stacey_abrams_doesnt_win_in_georgia_republicans_stole_it.html; State of the Union, *Abrams Won't Say Kemp Is Legitimate Governor*, CNN (video, n.d.; last accessed May 7, 2019), https://www.cnn.com/videos/politics/2018/11/18/stacey-abrams-brian-kemp-legitimate-georgia-governor-bts-sotu-vpx.cnn.

24. Bernie Sanders refused to call the Democratic primary process in 2016 "rigged" despite Donna Brazile's statements suggesting that the DNC worked with Hillary Clinton to assure her presidential nomination over Sanders. See the Nov. 8, 2017, Anderson Cooper CNN interview with Sanders posted at https://www.youtube.com/watch?v=VRoKgfoqmFQ and https://www.cnn.com/videos/politics/2017/11/09/bernie-sanders-responds-democratic-primary-rigged-against-him-sot-ac.cnn. Elizabeth Warren said the system was "rigged" for Clinton over Sanders. *Elizabeth Warren Agrees Democratic Race "Rigged" for Clinton*, BBC News, Nov. 3, 2017, https://www.bbc.com/news/world-us-canada-41850798. She then walked back the comment. Olivia Beavers, *Warren Walks Back Claim Democratic Primary Was Rigged*, The Hill, Nov. 9, 2017, https://thehill.com/homenews/senate/359645-warren-walks-back-claim-democratic-primary-was-rigged.

25. Richard L. Hasen, *Why Democrats Should Not Call the Georgia Governor's Race "Stolen,"* Slate, Nov. 18, 2018, https://slate.com/news-and-politics/2018/11/georgia-stacey-abrams-brian-kemp-election-not-stolen.html.

26. @ABFalecbaldwin, Twitter, Nov. 18, 2018, 4:27 p.m. PST, https://twitter.com/ABFalecbaldwin/status/1064314070558494720 [https://perma.cc/7UKT-KLT3].

27. @PattyArquette, Twitter, Nov. 19, 2018, 11:23 a.m. PST, https://twitter.com/PattyArquette/status/1064600076058849281 [https://perma.cc/8WJ6-FTMV]; @ulitave, Twitter, Nov. 19, 2018, 4:06 p.m. PST, https://twitter.com/ulitave/status/1064671351645134850 [https://perma.cc/Y7KA-A8AJ]; @thefool37, Twitter, Nov. 19, 2018, 12:35 p.m. PST, https://twitter.com/TheFool37/status/1064618140355694597 [https://perma.cc/X8NP-7BJZ].

28. The next few paragraphs draw from that *Slate* piece.

29. Annie Karni & Maggie Haberman, *Emboldened by His Attorney General, Trump Confronts Mueller Report Head-on*, N.Y. Times, Apr. 14, 2019, https://www.nytimes.com/2019/04/14/us/politics/trump-mueller-report.html. See also Special Counsel Robert S. Mueller III, *Report on the Investigation into Russian Interference in the 2016 Presidential Election*, vol. 2, at 8 (Mar. 2019) ("while this report does not conclude that the President committed a crime, it also does not exonerate him"). The official version appears at https://www.justice.gov/storage/report.pdf, and a searchable version appears at https://www.documentcloud.org/documents/5955379-Redacted-Mueller-Report.html#document/ [https://perma.cc/9TEW-JD3Z].

30. Donesha Aldridge, *Hillary Clinton: Abrams Would've Won if She Had a Fair Election*, 11Alive, Nov. 14, 2018, https://www.11alive.com/article/news/politics/elections/hillary-clinton-abrams-wouldve-won-if-she-had-a-fair-election/85-ff62e9b6–2172–4cd0-a5c0–651261fa1a4b [https://perma.cc/8G3W-WC9G]; @kamalaharris, Twitter, May 5, 2019, 5:45 p.m. PST, https://twitter.com/KamalaHarris/status/1125199779481436160 [https://perma.cc/25JQ-NJ79]; Ari Berman, *Brian Kemp's Win in Georgia Is Tainted by Voter Suppression*, Mother Jones, Nov. 16, 2018, https://www.motherjones.com/politics/2018/11/brian-kemps-win-in-georgia-tainted-by-voter-suppression-stacey-abrams/.

31. Rashaan Ayesh, *Stacey Abrams Calls Georgia's GOP Governor an "Architect of Voter Suppression,"* Axios, Apr. 3, 2019, https://www.axios.com/stacy-abrams-calls-georgias-gop-governor-architect-voter-suppression-e94f4dec-42e9-4057-8d6e-6b6d494c29a1.html [https://perma.cc/5THW-NFYA]; @adamkelsey, Twitter, Mar. 14, 2019, 1:03 p.m. PST, https://twitter.com/adamkelsey/status/1106284755610488833 [https://perma.cc/EDP9-AXDN].

32. Richard L. Hasen, *Stacey Abrams' New Lawsuit Against Georgia's Broken Voting System Is Incredibly Smart*, Slate, Nov. 27, 2018, https://slate.com/news-and-politics/2018/11/stacey-abrams-georgia-voting-rights-lawsuit.html.

33. Shaun Bowler, Thomas Brunell, Todd Donovan, & Paul Gronke, *Election Administration and Perceptions of Fair Elections*, 38 Electoral Stud. 1, 607 (2015).

34. Michael W. Sances & Charles Stewart III, *Partisanship and Confidence in the Vote Count: Evidence from U.S. National Elections since 2000*, 40 Electoral Stud. 176, 184–85 (2015).

Chapter 5. Surviving 2020 and Beyond

1. Glenn Thrush, *Pelosi Warns Democrats: Stay in the Center or Trump May Contest Election Results*, N.Y. Times, May 4, 2019, https://www.nytimes.com/2019/05/04/us/politics/nancy-pelosi.html.

2. Matt Zapotosky et al., *Michael Cohen Concludes His Testimony: "I Will Not Sit Back,"* Wash. Post, Feb. 27, 2019, https://www.washingtonpost.com/world/national-security/michael-cohen-testimony/2019/02/27/089664f0–39fb-11e9-a2cd-307b06d0257b_story.html.

3. Matt Zapotosky et al., *Cohen Tells Congress Trump Knew about Wikileaks Plans, Directed Hush Money Payments*, Wash. Post, Feb. 27, 2019, https://www.washingtonpost.com/politics/cohen-tells-congress-trump-knew-about-wikileaks-plans-directed-hush-money-payments/2019/02/27/f2784a20–3acd-11e9-a2cd-307b06d0257b_story.html; John Wagner, *Trump Renews Attacks on Media as "the True Enemy of the People,"* Wash. Post, Oct. 29, 2018, https://www.washingtonpost.com/politics/trump-renews-attacks-on-media-as-the-true-enemy-of-the-people/2018/10/29/9ebc62ee-db60–11e8–85df-7a6b4d25cfbb_story.html.

4. David A. Graham, *Do Republicans Actually Want to Postpone the 2020 Election?* Atlantic, Aug. 10, 2017, https://www.theatlantic.com/politics/archive/2017/08/poll-republicans/536472/; @kayleighmcenany, Twitter, Mar. 4, 2019, 6:13 p.m. PST, https://twitter.com/kayleighmcenany/status/1102754054587985921/ [https://perma.cc/JC96–4PRE]; @realdonaldtrump, Twitter, Feb. 9, 2019, 6:30 a.m. PST, https://twitter.com/realdonaldtrump/status/1094242164857556992 [https://perma.cc/58V7–7Z8Q]; Felicia Sonmez, *Trump Again Jokes about Staying on as President for More Than Two Terms*, Wash. Post, Apr. 18, 2019, https://www.washingtonpost.com/politics/trump-again-jokes-about-staying-on-as-president-for-more-than-two-terms/2019/04/18/05a5afce-6207–11e9–9ff2-abc984dc9eec_story.html.

5. Mattathias Schwartz, Intelligencer, *Obama Had a Secret Plan in Case Trump Rejected 2016 Election Results*, New York, Oct. 10, 2018, http://nymag.com/intelligencer/2018/10/obama-had-a-secret-plan-in-case-trump-rejected-2016-results.html.

6. Steven Levitsky & Daniel Ziblatt, *How Democracies Die* 21–22, 176–203, 223 (2018).

7. Rob Whitley, *Is "Trump Derangement Syndrome" a Real Mental Condition?* Psychology Today, Jan. 4, 2019, https://www.psychologytoday.com/us/blog/talking-about-men/201901/is-trump-derangement-syndrome-real-mental-condition.

8. Norman J. Ornstein, *Our Elections Are Wide-Open for a Constitutional Crisis*, Wash. Post, Oct. 26, 2018, https://www.washingtonpost.com/opinions/our-elections-are-wide-open-for-a-constitutional-crisis/2018/10/26/317cb7e0-d86a-11e8–83a2-d1c3da28d6b6_story.html/.

9. On the polarization of the judiciary, see Richard L. Hasen, *Polarization and the Judiciary*, 22 Ann. Rev. Pol. Sci. 261 (2019), https://doi.org/10.1146/annurev-polisci-051317-125141. On Democratic frustration with the Supreme Court nomination process leading to calls to pack the Court, see Carl Hulse, *Frustrated Democrats Intensify Demand for Big Institutional Changes*, N.Y. Times, Mar. 27, 2019, https://www.nytimes.com/2019/03/27/us/politics/democrats-filibuster-court-packing.html.

10. American Law Institute, *Principles of the Law, Election Administration: Non-precinct Voting and Resolution of Ballot Counting Disputes*, part 3, *Procedures for the Resolution of a Disputed Presidential Election* (2019), https://www.ali.org/publications/show/resolution-election-disputes/.

11. On Democrats campaigning on voter suppression issues, see Trip Gabriel, *Voting Issues and Gerrymanders Are Now Key Political Battlegrounds*, N.Y. Times, Jan. 2, 2019, https://www.nytimes.com/2019/01/02/us/politics/voting-gerrymander-elections.html. On Moral Mondays, see Anne Blythe, *"We Will Continue to Resist." 5 Years After First Moral Monday, Their Fight Continues*, News & Observer, Apr. 30, 2018, https://www.newsobserver.com/latest-news/article210185774.html.

12. *Elections in America: Concerns over Security, Divisions over Expanding Access to Voting*, Pew Research Center, Oct. 29, 2018, http://www.people-press.org/2018/10/29/elections-in-america-concerns-over-security-divisions-over-expanding-access-to-voting/ [https://perma.cc/7Q35–6Q7P].

13. On the work of ERIC, see Electronic Registration Information Center, *2017 Annual Report*, https://ericstates.org/wp-content/uploads/2019/01/FINAL_ERIC_2017_Annual_Report.pdf [https://perma.cc/X84A-VH2F]. The Bipartisan Policy Center is continuing much of the work of the Bauer-Ginsberg Presidential Commission on Election Administration, and its work in this area is posted at https://bipartisanpolicy.org/blog/tag/

presidential-commission-on-election-administration/. The full Bauer-Ginsberg final report and supporting materials are posted at http://web.mit.edu/supportthevoter/www/.

14. Press release, *Commissioners Hovland, Palmer Sworn in to Restore Quorum at EAC*, U.S. Election Assistance Commission, Feb. 6, 2019, https://www.eac.gov/news/2019/02/06/commissioners-hovland-palmer-sworn-in-to-restore-quorum-at-eac/ [https://perma.cc/3PUU-B4E9]; Jacqueline Thomsen, *Election Agency Prepares to Tackle Foreign Interference*, The Hill, Dec. 24, 2018, https://thehill.com/policy/cybersecurity/422563-election-agency-prepares-to-tackle-foreign-interference; Rick Hasen, *Matthew Masterson, Blocked for EAC Reappointment by Speaker Paul Ryan, Will Continue to Work on Cybersecurity Issues for DHS*, Election Law Blog, Mar. 26, 2018, https://electionlawblog.org/?p=98353 [https://perma.cc/PXG6-TQNF]. On Palmer, see Tierney Sneed, *Court Docs: US Elections Commission Member Helped with Sketchy Fraud Report*, Talking Points Memo, May 22, 2019, https://talkingpointsmemo.com/muckraker/voter-fraud-report-aliens-invasion-donald-palmer.

15. On the potential issues with the auditability of BMDs, see Andrew Appel, Richard DeMillo, & Philip Stark, Ballot-Marking Devices (BMDs) Cannot Assure the Will of the Voters (unpublished draft dated Apr. 21, 2019, available at https://papers.ssrn.com/sol3/papers.cfm?abstract_id=3375755).

16. Jessica Huseman, *How the Election Assistance Commission Came Not to Care So Much about Election Security*, ProPublica, Nov. 5, 2018, https://www.propublica.org/article/election-assistance-commission-came-not-to-care-so-much-about-election-security; Christy McCormick, *Securing the Accuracy and Efficiency of Elections*, Wash. Times, Mar. 3, 2019, https://www.washingtontimes.com/news/2019/mar/3/despite-the-efforts-of-russia-and-others-no-hacker/ [https://perma.cc/XS5L-WHSD]; @jessicahuseman, Twitter, Mar. 3, 2019, 5:23 p.m. PST, https://twitter.com/JessicaHuseman/status/1102378941166338048 [https://perma.cc/J58T-99FR] ("At last count, I'd asked EAC Chairwoman Christy McCormick or a spokesperson 14 times if she had rethought her initial denial that Russia intervened in the 2016 election. Now in the Washington Times she finally admits she has.").

In McCormick's *Washington Times* op-ed, she wrongly wrote that election administration is "an area that historically and constitutionally rests solely with the states." In fact, the Elections Clause gives Congress broad power to set cybersecurity and other rules for federal elections even if states object. See Franita Tolson, *Election Law "Federalism" and the Limits of the Antidiscrimination Framework*, 59 Wm. & Mary L. Rev. 2211 (2018).

17. Eric A. Fischer, *In Focus: The Designation of Election Systems as Critical Infrastructure*, Congressional Research Service, updated Jan. 28, 2019, https://fas.org/sgp/crs/misc/IF10677.pdf [https://perma.cc/D9FX-C8V6]; Wendy Underhill, *Many Are Critical of DHS Designation of Elections as Critical Infrastructure*, NCSL Blog, Jan. 11, 2017, http://www.ncsl.org/blog/2017/01/11/many-are-critical-of-dhs-designation-of-elections-as-critical-infrastructure.aspx [https://perma.cc/K75R-67HL].

18. For some of my tentative thinking on these questions, see Richard L. Hasen, *Cheap Speech and What It Has Done (to American Democracy)*, 16 First Amend. L. Rev. 200 (2017–18), https://falrunc.files.wordpress.com/2018/03/falr-volume-16-symposium-issue3.pdf#page=89.

19. On the role of Facebook, Google, and others in incorporating fact checks into material appearing online, see Alexios Mantzarlis, Daniel Funke, & Susan Benkelman, *How Fact-Checking Has Changed since 2015*, Poynter, Feb. 14, 2019, https://www.poynter.org/fact-checking/2019/how-fact-checking-has-changed-since-2015/ [https://perma.cc/A65M-DVMC].

20. Will Oremus, *The Temptation of Apple News*, Slate, Sept. 25, 2018, https://slate.com/technology/2018/09/apple-news-media-slate-ad-sales-no-money.html; Lucas Shaw, *Google, Facebook Lead Digital March to Half of U.S. Ad Market*, Bloomberg, Sept. 20, 2018, https://www.bloomberg.com/news/articles/2018-09-20/google-facebook-lead-digital-s-march-to-half-of-u-s-ad-market.

21. John Wildermuth & Tal Kopan, *California's Late Votes Broke Big for Democrats. Here's Why GOP Was Surprised*, S.F. Chronicle, Nov. 30, 2018, https://www.sfchronicle.com/politics/article/California-s-late-votes-broke-big-for-13432727.php.

22. Richard L. Hasen, *The Voting Wars: From Florida 2000 to the Next Election Meltdown* 197 (2012).

23. *Id.* at 199.

24. On "red state" and "blue state" election law, see Richard L. Hasen, *Election Law's Path in the Roberts Court's First Decade: A Sharp Right Turn but with Speed Bumps and Surprising Twists*, 68 Stan. L. Rev. 1597, 1601 (2016). On automatic voter registration, see Brennan Center for Justice, Automatic Voter Registration, https://www.brennancenter.org/analysis/automatic-voter-registration [https://perma.cc/F62Z-7LNC] ("AVR makes two simple, yet transformative, changes to the way our country has traditionally registered voters. First, AVR makes voter registration 'opt-out' instead of 'opt-in'—eligible citizens who interact with government agencies are registered to vote or have their existing registration information updated, unless they affirmatively decline. Again, the voter can opt-out; it is not compulsory registration.

Second, those agencies transfer voter registration information electronically to election officials instead of using paper registration forms.").

25. On the difficult task of balancing free expression and preventing the spread of disinformation, hate speech, and other harmful speech, see David Kaye, *Speech Police: The Global Struggle to Govern the Internet* 116–30 (2019).

Index